The Cathedral Builders

Frontispiece (overleaf):
The Legend of St Barbara by Van Eyck (*1437*).
To the right of the octagonal tower is a
stonemason's lodge. (Antwerp Museum.)
The spire of Notre-Dame de Paris, built by
Viollet-le-Duc.

The Cathedral Builders

by Jean Gimpel

Translated by Teresa Waugh

HarperPerennial
A Division of HarperCollins*Publishers*

First Harper Colophon edition published 1984. First HarperPerennial edition published 1992.

Library of Congress Cataloging-in-Publication Data
Gimpel, Jean.
    The cathedral builders.

    (Harper colophon books)
    Translation of: Les bâtisseurs de cathédrales.
    Reprint. Originally published: New York : Grove Press, 1983.
    Bibliography: p.
    Includes index.
    1. Cathedrals. 2. Architecture, Medieval. 3. Christian art and symbolism—Medieval, 500-1500. I. Title.
NA4830.G5313   1984   726'.6'094   84-47572
ISBN 0-06-091158-1 (pbk.)

92 93 94 95 96 CW 10 9 8 7 6 5 4 3 2 1

Contents

The Cathedral Builders

The Medieval Miracle

In three centuries – from *1050* to *1350* – several million tons of stone were quarried in France for the building of *80* cathedrals, *500* large churches and some tens of thousands of parish churches. More stone was excavated in France during these three centuries than at any time in Ancient Egypt, although the volume of the Great Pyramid alone is *2,500,000* cubic metres. The foundations of the cathedrals are laid as deep as *10* metres (the average depth of a Paris underground station) and in some cases there is as much stone below ground as can be seen above.

In the Middle Ages there was a church or chapel for every *200* inhabitants or thereabouts, so the area covered by Christian churches was quite considerable in relation to the modest size of the towns; it is known that in Norwich, Lincoln and York, cities with a population of between five and ten thousand, there were respectively fifty, forty-nine and forty-one churches and chapels. The ambitious who wanted to rebuild and enlarge their churches were confronted with serious problems: one or two neighbouring churches often had to be demolished and homes had to be built for the dispossessed householders.

The size of the cathedral at Amiens, which covered *7,700* square metres, made it possible for the entire population of the city – some ten thousand people – to attend

The spire of Notre-Dame de Paris, built by
Viollet-le-Duc.

one ceremony. In modern terms, this would mean building a stadium large enough to seat a million people in the heart of any city with a population of one million. The largest stadium in the world today can only seat 240,000.

The height of naves, towers and spires is startling. A fourteen-floor building could be erected in the choir of Beauvais Cathedral without reaching the vaulting, which is 48 metres high. In order to compete with the people of twelfth-century Chartres who built their spire 105 metres high, the present municipality would have to build a thirty-floor skyscraper; and a forty-floor skyscraper would be needed to equal the spire at Strasbourg, which reaches to 142 metres.

There is no shortage of documentation concerning the builders of these vast churches, and yet it is rare for historical truth to be so clouded in legend: legends of guilds, of secrets, of voluntary labour and of builder-monks. For over fifty years French historians and archaeologists have, with one notable exception, abandoned the study of the history of building and have concentrated on aspects which, though interesting, are so specialized that there has been no comprehensive view of the problems presented by medieval architecture.

It was not the same in the nineteenth century and at the beginning of the twentieth century, when some great French historians considered the subject as a whole – Jules Quicherat, Victor Mortet and above all Viollet-le-Duc, whom until very recently it was fashionable to denigrate. A closer look at his *Entretiens sur l'architecture* and his *Dictionnaire* will prove him to be one of the most outstanding figures of the nineteenth century. Clearly he made mistakes, but who does not? His knowledge of medieval society and of the history of building is remarkable to this day. He is blamed for having rebuilt the Château de Pierrefonds with a degree of brutishness. This is fair, but the state of ruin into which the *château* had fallen when Napoleon III ordered its restoration must not be overlooked. Without Viollet-le-Duc's dynamism, many of the buildings which we admire today would be no more. He has been reproached for his excesses, but we may well ask whether the next century will blame our restorers for having spent too little on laboratory tests to discover the causes of the prevalent dramatic stone disease.

Pierre du Colombier, a first-class historian, is the exception mentioned above. He was not even a medievalist but in 1953 he published a remarkable work, *Les Chantiers des Cathédrales*, which is just as interesting to the general public as to specialists, for whom it is an excellent reference book.

But whereas French research has, for the most part, tended to ignore this field up to now, German, English and American scholars have continued the work of the nineteenth century. German scholars have particularly studied their own fourteenth- and fifteenth-century buildings – the fourteenth and fifteenth centuries being the great period for construction in Germany. Their conclusions must, however, be treated carefully with reference to the twelfth and thirteenth centuries, since a transformation of working conditions occurred in Europe and especially in France during the second half of the thirteenth century.

On the other hand, work undertaken in England and the United States over the last fifty years by G. G. Coulton, J. Harvey, L. F. Salzman, H. M. Colvin, F. Bucher, L.-R. Shelby and above all D. Knoop and G. P. Jones in *The Medieval Mason* and in the review *Ars Quatuor Coronatorum* gives us a better understanding of life on the site during the 'cathedral crusade' and makes it easier to distinguish legend from truth. These writers recognize the importance of the right to work; they have studied in some detail the evolution of the workers' masonry and have pinpointed the role played by monks in the building of their abbeys. Mention must also be made of H. Kraus, an American living in Paris who in 1979 published a book called *Gold Was the Mortar* on the financing of eight European cathedrals. It is one of the paradoxes of the twentieth century that whereas political news is instantly broadcast throughout the world and scientific information is rapidly disseminated, the results of historical research often have to wait for years before they travel. In defense of historians, it must be appreciated that in this instance it can be difficult, not to say impossible, to obtain some of these works. For instance, the review *Ars Quatuor Coronatorum*, which includes some articles of prime importance, is published in London by the Masonic Lodge 2076 and is therefore never on sale publicly, nor can it be found in any public library. This seems a shame, because this Lodge has made a careful and methodical study of certain aspects of medieval building and has particularly analyzed the accounts of the civil and religious building sites of the thirteenth and fourteenth centuries in England.

All histories of medieval architecture make the classic distinction between Romanesque and Gothic buildings and they agree that the change took place in the middle of the twelfth century. This distinction presupposes that the Gothic style was typified by certain specific characteristics such as the flying buttress or rib vaulting. Now many Gothic churches were built without flying buttresses and it has finally been acknowledged that the famous rib vaulting is not as important as was formerly thought.

There is no fundamental distinction between a Romanesque building and a Gothic one, but there is a vast difference between a mid-twelfth-century church and one built at the end of the thirteenth century, and this difference results from an accumulation of hundreds of small technical discoveries due to the ingenuity of the architects and builders of cathedrals. There was no such thing as a Romanesque or Gothic cathedral builder, any more than there were Romanesque or Gothic workshops: there were simply creative builders and others who slavishly copied old techniques. And this is something which must be stressed.

It is an astonishing fact that for 250 years, from the end of the thirteenth to the beginning of the sixteenth century, the period in which the transepts of Sens, Senlis and Beauvais were built, no technical progress was made in construction. Late Gothic is characterized merely by ornamentation superimposed on a technical framework which was perfected between the eleventh and thirteenth centuries. There were 250 years of invention, followed by 250 years when men were satisfied with copying their predecessors. This standstill in architectural development at the end of the thirteenth century is part of a phenomenon concerning all aspects of medieval history, be it religious, technical, economic, social or psychological. Perhaps it can be said that a somewhat similar phenomenon is occuring at the end of this twentieth century. The simple lines of the technically revolutionary architecture of, for instance, Le Corbusier, Gropius and Mies van der Rohe are being succeeded throughout the world by a style that makes decorative use of their structural revolution. It would seem that the arbitrary separation of the Romanesque and the Gothic, in the middle of the twelfth century, corresponds to no particular turning point in medieval history, whereas the second half of the thirteenth century is of marked importance in the history of the Middle Ages.

The period from 1050 until the second half of the thirteenth century was a period of dynamism and ascendancy for Christian Europe in general and for France in particular. It was an age of creation in which some of the greatest spirits of the Western world were to worship, teach or rule – St Bernard, Abélard, St Francis of Assisi, St Thomas Aquinas, Roger Bacon, St Louis – whilst the cathedral builders erected these extraordinary churches which were to bear witness to the highest peak of medieval Christianity.

If a date had to be chosen to symbolize the ending of the dynamic and spiritual impetus of this society, it would be 1277, the year of the doctrinal condemnations pronounced by the Bishop of Paris, and the year in which Thomism became confused with Averroism. Gabriel Le Bras wrote on this subject: 'For half a century, from 1227 to 1277, canon law was at its most powerful, and . . . the decline of medieval Christianity was heralded by the new states of mind and feelings which canon law was trying to suppress: revolt against the established church, affirmations of independence by civilian societies, evolution of the plastic arts and sacred music.' We will have occasion to return to this general crisis after which the Western world was to move definitively into the modern age, long before what has come to be known as the Renaissance.

Saint Bernard and Suger

The spread of Christianity and the history of the builders are linked to the development of the monastic orders. St Benedict, the founder of Monte Cassino, formulated, in the sixth century, a Rule of Life which was to spread with remarkable speed. By degrees there were to be Benedictine monasteries all over Europe. This Rule of St Benedict can be regarded as one of the great historical events of the Middle Ages. It organized spiritual life and manual work around the seven canonical hours with a sense of balance which was to be its strength. But at certain periods observance of the Rule lapsed and the Benedictine order had to be reformed. Two of these reforms are of interest to us : the Cluniac reform in the tenth century, and the Cîteaux reform in the twelfth century.

The Cluniac reform took place after raids by the Saracens, the Normans and the Hungarians had prevented the development of the Carolingian Renaissance and had thrown the life of the Benedictine monks into disarray and immorality. At the beginning of the tenth century, the Duke of Aquitaine, William the Pius, founded a monastery at Cluny, a small village in the Mâconnais. And here the amazing spirit of Cluny, which was to have so marked a civilizing influence on the Western world, was born. Within a few years, in a world of feudalism and brutality, Cluniac monks had spread throughout Europe, from Poland to Portugal, with some 1,400 monasteries and dependencies.

In order to keep in touch with his abbots and priors, the Senior Abbot of Cluny convoked assemblies at frequent intervals where representatives of monasteries came to report on the state of each community and to receive instructions. In order to lodge the hundreds of delegates from all over France, Spain or Hungary, the Abbot of Cluny had ceaselessly to enlarge his monastery. At the beginning of the twelfth century the abbey could house 400 monks and 2,000 visitors. The church, built between 1088 and 1135, was on the same scale, for we know that this vast abbey church, which was almost completely destroyed in Napoleonic times, was as large as St Peter's in Rome.

The science of construction in Western Europe advanced considerably as a result of the problems presented by the building of some 1,400 Cluniac monasteries. The first abbeys were built of wood as practically no one knew the

Cluny: all that has survived from the
vandalism of the early nineteenth century.
The Holy-Water Tower and the Clocktower.

whereabouts of good quarries, nor how to cut stone. St Odilo, the Senior Abbot of Cluny, confirmed this when he said : 'I found an abbey of wood and I leave one of marble.' He had had antique marble columns carried up the Durance and the Rhône. In order to attract travellers to Spain on the Santiago de Compostela pilgrimage and in order to interest Europe in the Christian reconquest of Spain, which was occupied by the Moors, Cluny was to encourage the building and enlargement of vast basilicas along this route.

The Cluniac order played an important part in the reform of the Church: Gregory VII, the great eleventh-century pope, was to depend on Cluny for support, and Urban II, who in 1096 preached the First Crusade, came out of Cluny. At the head of the order are to be found men like St Hugh, one of the most perfect examples of the monastic ideal, and Peter the Venerable, the last Grand Abbot of Cluny, who in his genius had the Koran translated with geographical and historical references to Islamic beliefs, so that he could fight the Muslim world on an intellectual plane.

By the end of the eleventh century the strict observance of St Benedict's Rule had lapsed among Cluniac monks. And in 1098 St Robert, the Abbot of Molesmes, founded a monastery for the reform of the Rule in the middle of the swampy forest of Cîteaux in the diocese of Langres. This new order at Cîteaux came into its own when St Bernard, a local young nobleman, came with some friends to join the Abbot of Molesmes in 1112. By the time St Bernard died in 1152, the order included 343 monasteries, and before the end of the twelfth century there were 530.

St Bernard, who was the soul and inspiration of the order, organized the Second Crusade from 1147 and was the political arbiter of Europe as well as the unofficial head of Christendom. St Bernard's determination to apply the Rule of St Benedict in all its rigour was to have important spiritual, social, economic and technical consequences. The success of Cluny was due to the will of pious and energetic men who wanted to wrench Christian Europe from the barbarism of the tenth and eleventh centuries. The success of Cîteaux was due to a group of men who in their desire for austerity wanted to wean the West from the vanity and worldly pleasures that were beginning to predominate.

Since the fall of the Roman Empire, the economy of Europe had been a closed one, but contact with the East, resulting from the commercial ventures of Italian cities and from the First Crusade, drew attention to her needs. Society envied the precious stones, ivories, scents and beautiful silks of the Orient.

St Bernard and his companions withdrew from the world where this taste for luxury was overtaking the love of God, even among the Cluniacs. Perhaps in order to protect itself from worldly temptation, or in order more easily to devote itself entirely to God, the Cistercian order insisted that its monks remove themselves from towns and that they live in the depths of forests. Having reclaimed several thousands of acres of land and created model farms by means which contrasted strongly with feudal artisans' methods, the Cistercians set about building their vast abbeys.

The austerity of the order was reflected in its buildings. There were no porches, no towers, there was no sculpture and no stained glass. Whereas the Cluniac churches were covered with gold and paint. the Cistercian churches were white. The bare stone was left unadorned

In a famous letter addressed to the Cluniacs, St Bernard spoke out against the richly coloured Cluniac churches:

O vanity of vanities, but more folly than vanity! Every part of the church shines, but the poor man is hungry! The church walls are clothed in gold, while the children of the church remain naked . . . Tell me then, poor monks – if indeed you are poor – what is gold doing in the holy place? To speak plainly, greed is the root of all evil, greed, the slave of idols . . . for the sight of these sumptuous and amazing vanities encourages man to give rather than to pray. So riches attract riches, money attracts money. Why, I do not know, but the greater the abundance of riches, the more willingly men give. The eye is dazzled by gifts of golden roofs to house relics and purse-strings are unloosed. Beautiful statues of saints are thought more venerable if they are richly painted. The faithful come to kiss them and are encouraged to give. They are more concerned with the beauty of the statues than with the virtue of the saints . . . A man at prayer seems even to have forgotten the purpose of his prayer . . . The poor are allowed to groan in hunger and the money they need is spent on useless luxury.

St Bernard's polemics had only a limited influence on Cluniac extravagance, and at the time of his death the General Chapters of the Cistercians themselves had to remind some abbots of the statutes regarding the decoration of their monasteries. But such was St Bernard's personality that during his lifetime no one, of whatever moral standing in the Christian Church, could avoid seeking his approval. Thus the great builder, the Abbot Suger, Regent of France during the absence of Louis VII on a crusade, wrote two books to justify his love of splendour which was manifest in the rebuilding of the Benedictine Abbey of Saint-Denis. These books explain what it was that urged the men of this period to devote so much to building.

Unlike most great men of the day, Suger was of humble origin, and he never concealed this fact. He was probably the son of a serf. At the age of eleven he was admitted to the school of Saint-Denis-de-l'Estrée, where he was brought up in the shadow of the abbey with the sons of the nobility and the princes of the blood. It was here that he made friends with the future King of France. He recalls that from his earliest youth his ambition was to rebuild Saint-Denis : 'I did it so much more willingly because it was something that since my schooldays I had wanted to do if it were ever possible.'

For several centuries Saint-Denis had been the Royal Abbey where the Kings

Saint-Denis: Suger at Christ's feet in the tympanum over the central doorway.

of France were buried. There, piously preserved, were the relics of St Denis and of his two legendary companions, St Rustique and St Eleuthere, whom Suger called 'the holy martyrs'.

Suger was sent on several missions to Rome, where he contributed towards strengthening the ties, at that time very tenuous, between the papacy and the King of France. There, in 1121, he learnt one day that he had been nominated Abbot of Saint-Denis; he returned to France and immediately began to lead a life of luxury. St Bernard, as ever concerned about the dignity of the Church, strongly criticized the attitude of the new abbot, who, accepting the reproof of the Abbot of Clairvaux, moderated his way of life and undertook the reform of the abbey, which had become very lax.

In 1127 St Bernard wrote Suger a somewhat surprising letter, in which he congratulated him on having mended his ways and went on to express his wish that a certain monk, Étienne de Garlande, who had become seneschal, be withdrawn from the royal favour. By the end of the year Étienne de Garlande had been removed from power and St Bernard found himself for the first time in direct and official contact with the King of France. From that time St Bernard and Suger, although of very different temperaments, were in agreement. They both knew that it was in their interests not to oppose each other; one was the unofficial representative of the papacy, the other the most important political figure in the kingdom of France.

Nevertheless, Suger, whose passion for riches and splendour was boundless and who carried the taste for lavish decoration and ceremony even further than the Cluniacs, wrote in order to avert an attack from St Bernard :

Let every man follow his own opinion. As for myself, I declare that it has always seemed right to me that everything which is most precious should above all add to the celebration of the Holy Eucharist. If golden cups, golden phials and small golden mortars were used, in obedience to the Word of God and by the command of the Prophet, to contain the blood of he-goats, calves or red heifers, how much more should they be used to hold the blood of Jesus Christ? . . . Should we dispose of the golden vases and precious stones and all that creation holds most valuable? . . . Those who criticize us [Suger was always thinking of St Bernard] claim that this celebration needs only a holy soul, a pure mind and faithful intention. We are certainly in complete agreement that these are what matter above all else. But we believe that outward ornaments and sacred chalices should serve nowhere so much as in our worship, and this with all inward purity and all outward nobility.

Suger then covered his main altar with gold. 'We have entirely enclosed it,' he said, 'by placing on each side of the existing altar golden panels, and by adding a fourth which is even more precious, so that it seems to be entirely surrounded in gold.'

But Suger was not the only one who wanted magnificence and splendour, for so did the Holy Martyrs. When Suger was considering placing a modest altar before the tomb of St Denis and his companions, the saints themselves demanded the very best : 'Whilst I, through weakness and pusillanimity, had planned a modest altar-piece, the Holy Martyrs themselves procured in a most unexpected way much gold and stones so precious that even kings would be unlikely to own them. It was as though they wished to tell us through their own mouths, "Whether you wish it or not, we want the very best."'

Thus encouraged, Suger had no more worries and he abandoned himself to the pleasure of acquiring the most magnificent objects. He described the masterpieces which were to be placed on the main altar, some of which are still to be seen in the Louvre. 'We have adapted for use on the altar a porphyry vase, beautifully carved and polished . . . and changed it from the amphora which it was into the shape of an eagle decorated with gold and silver . . . We have acquired a precious chalice made from one huge piece of sardonyx . . . also another vase made from the same stone but of a different shape, more resembling an amphora . . . and yet another vessel which seems to be made of beryl or crystal.'

Above and at right: Objets acquired by
Suger for the high altar at Saint-Denis.
At present in the Louvre.

It was as a result of divine intervention that some monks brought him the
precious stones which he needed to decorate the seven-metre-high cross, the
true monument to theological science which he placed in the choir and which
could be seen from every corner of the church.

We do not wish to remain silent about a droll but remarkable miracle which the
Lord granted us in this matter. Just as I had come to a halt through lack of
precious stones, and had no possibility of procuring enough (their rarity making
them very expensive), lo and behold [some monks] from Cîteaux, from another
Cistercian monastery and from Fontevrault appeared in the small room next to
the church and offered to sell us an abundance of precious stones : amethysts,
sapphires, rubies, emeralds and topazes such as I could not have hoped to

12

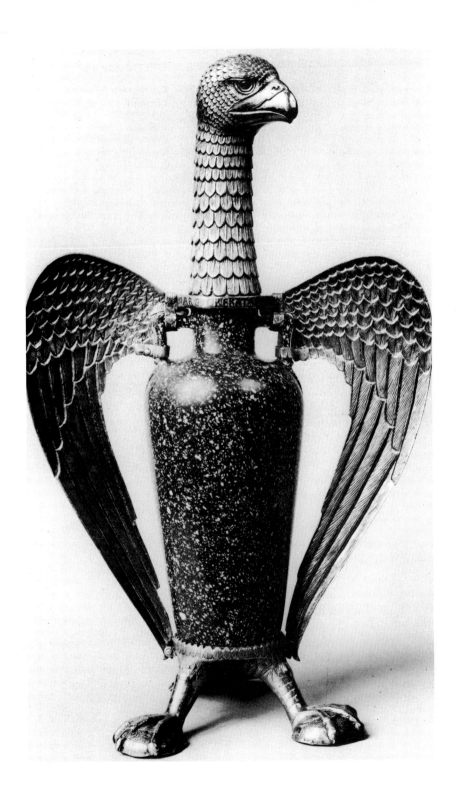

collect with a space of ten years. They had been given them as alms by the Comte Thibaud . . . As for ourselves, freed from the worry of searching for precious stones, we gave thanks to God and to the monks we gave four hundred pounds although the jewels were worth more. And it was not these alone, but quantities of other gems and pearls which richly served to perfect so holy an ornament. If I remember rightly, we used some eighty marks of fine gold. We were able to have finished within a space of two years the pedestal decorated with the four evangelists, the column with the Holy Image enamelled and worked with extreme delicacy, as well as the life of Our Lord with the allegorical figures from the Old Testament and the death of the Saviour on the capital. This was all the work of several goldsmiths from Lorraine – sometimes five, sometimes seven.

So that these sacred objects might be sufficiently admired and venerated by the faithful, the choir of Saint-Denis had to be suitably lighted. Suger knocked down the dark Carolingian basilica and built around the relics, the altars and the great cross a choir with large windows. Delighted with the effect he had achieved, he then drew up an inscription to the glory of Light which he had engraved inside the church :

> With the new chevet attached to the old façade
> The heart of the sanctuary glows in splendour.
> That which is united in splendour, radiates in splendour
> And the magnificent work inundated with a new light shines.
> It is I, Suger, who have in my time enlarged this edifice.
> Under my direction it was done.

The builders of Saint-Denis, like those who worked for the Cluniacs, had to submit to the demands which we have mentioned with regard to Suger, and the history of building is tied to the unceasing attempts of architects to make openings in the walls without compromising the solidity of the buildings. Many efforts to light the nave and the choir were more or less successful. Some buildings which were too audaciously contrived collapsed. The old Byzantine or Islamic architects had been more concerned with protecting the insides of buildings from the violence of the sunlight. Rarely until now had architects been called upon to build such vast edifices so far north as Burgundy or the Île-de-France.

There were other motives, besides, which drove Suger to devote himself so ardently and with such enthusiasm to the rebuilding of his abbey. While light is necessary for the worthy glorification of God, the largest possible number of the faithful must also be able, without jostling, to approach and contemplate the Holy Relics on feast days. The choir must be large enough for the mass of believers to circulate in an orderly fashion, and Suger, so as to prove the absolute need to enlarge the choir, describes with verve the tumultous scene on a feast day in the old basilica :

Saint-Denis: detail of the south doorway in the west façade.

Often, on a feast day, the basilica was so full that the crowd was overflowing through every doorway, and not only could those not enter who were trying to enter, but those who were already inside were forced back by those ahead of them, and obliged to go out. Sometimes, astounding though it may seem, there was such a thrusting back by the dense crowd against those who were doing their best to come in to venerate and kiss the holy relics – the Nail and Crown of Thorns of Our Lord – that no one among the tightly packed masses could move so much as a foot. There was no alternative but to stand still, transfixed like a marble statue; all that was possible was to scream. The agony of the women was such, and so unbearable, that, crushed as in a wine-press among a crowd of robust men, their faces seemed bloodless as at the thought of death. They uttered such terrible cries as though in childbirth, and many of them were pitifully trampled on. Some were carried shoulder high by men who, in pity, helped them and resolutely afforded them a base. Many held their breath, or gasped in total despair in the friars' garden. More than once, the friars who were showing visitors evidence of Our Lord's Passion were overcome by the anger and quarrelling of the crowds and, having no other way out, escaped through the windows with the relics.

It was important to put altars all around the choir so that each priest could celebrate mass. And Suger conceived the idea of radiating chapels, which were so practical that they were adopted in many churches in the second half of the century.

By making the church of the Kings of France so glorious, Suger greatly strengthened the King's prestige with his vassals. But his own self-esteem played a considerable part in the rebuilding of the abbey. He thanked God for having granted him the honour of reconstructing Saint-Denis and made allowances for money to be spent on a celebration in memory of himself in the abbey – an honour as yet reserved for the Kings alone.

Wishing to be remembered by posterity, he took steps which were at times almost comic but nevertheless effective, since his name has lived into the twentieth century. He had four likenesses of himself placed in the abbey and drew up thirteen inscriptions in his own honour which he had engraved in stone or in metal in various parts of the church. There is Suger at the feet of Christ in Majesty on the tympanum, there he is again at the feet of the Virgin Mary in a stained-glass window in the ambulatory; his name is written in the glass in letters as large as those which honour the Mother of God.

On the façade of Saint-Denis the following monumental inscription which recalls the part played by Suger and the date of the consecration of the narthex can still be seen :

In honour of the Church which nurtured and exalted him, Suger worked, rendering back to you your due, Saint Denis, martyr.

The choir of Saint-Denis rebuilt by Suger.

He prays that your prayers will obtain for him a place in Paradise.

In the year of the Word eleven hundred and forty the consecration took place.

On a ewer, which is now in the Louvre, he had the following lines engraved:

'Since it is our duty to offer libations to God in gold and gems, I, Suger, offer this vase to the Saviour.' And on the *Justa*, a fourth-century Egyptian work, he wrote: 'Eleanor, his wife, gave this vase to King Louis, Mitadolus had given it to her ancestor, the King gave it to me and Suger to the Saints.'

Suger's great triumph as a 'builder' was established on the second Sunday in June, 1144, the date of the consecration of the choir. This day, which he planned with his genius for organization, had perhaps a greater effect on architecture than any other day in history. To the grandiose ceremony to consecrate the twenty altars Suger summoned the King of France, all the peers of the realm, the archbishops and bishops, including those from Sens, Senlis, Soissons, Chartres, Rheims and Beauvais. Dazzled by the new abbey, they returned to their own cathedrals anxious to equal this extraordinary spiritual creation.

For centuries now Saint-Denis has been made so austere that, were Suger to return, he would no doubt suppose that the abbey had become Cistercian. St Bernard seems to have conquered Suger. Today the gilded altars, the Great Cross covered with precious stones, the chalices and other treasures have all disappeared. The walls have been whitewashed or left bare by recent restorers. The paint has been removed from the sculptures. The choirstalls, the paving, the multi-coloured hangings have all gone. Suger's colourful splendour is, for the most part, no more than a memory in modern day France. Equally the Cluniac abbeys and cathedrals which were conceived and built in the spirit of Cluny or of Suger are quite unrecognizable.

We can no longer appreciate this duality of the Christian world which was symbolized by St Bernard on the one hand and Suger on the other : we can only really understand the spirit of Cîteaux. The Cistercian monasteries, built away from towns, have remained austere. The walls remain bare, the windows are made of colourless glass and there is still no porch, no tower and no sculpture.

But it is important to ask why we can hardly even discover in Cluniac monuments and cathedrals traces of this medieval conception symbolized by Suger. What spiritual events and which material facts have hidden from us one whole aspect of the Christian spirit in the ascendant? It was certainly not St Bernard who won.

The introduction of Roman law at the end of the thirteenth century was to lead medieval society towards the Renaissance and modern times. This Renaissance was to be a rebirth of ancient thought. And the cult of Antiquity had a catastrophic effect on medieval monuments. If churches were not systematically destroyed in order to be replaced by others on classical lines, like the Pantheon in

'In honour of the Church which nurtured and exalted him...' Suger's inscription to his own glory on the west façade of Saint-Denis.

From the recumbent statues at Saint-Denis, Jean and Blanche, the children of St. Louis (thirteenth-century enamelled figures from the Abbey of Royaumont).

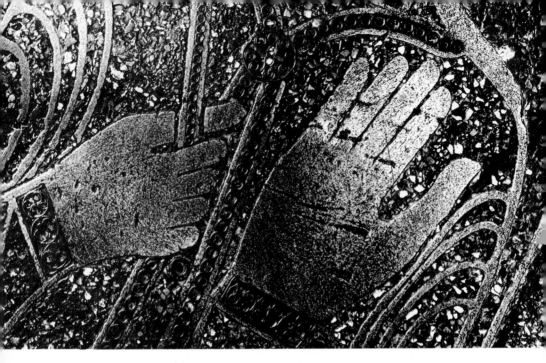

One of the treasures of Saint-Denis: mid-twelfth-century mosaic *cloisonné* slab depicting Frédégonde, Queen of Neustria (d. *597*) from the Abbey of Saint-Germain-des-Prés.

Paris, it was because of the vast expense such plans would have incurred. On the other hand, churches were transformed little by little to bring them in line with the taste of the day. The damage caused by the French Revolution of 1789 cannot compare with the barbarous destruction of the seventeenth century and, above all, the eighteenth. An inventory of the devastation of the eighteenth century would run to volumes. And it is an absolute scandal that guidebooks can continue to talk of the ravages of the Revolution without mentioning the other destruction of the eighteenth century. But the nineteenth and twentieth centuries themselves are responsible for the demolition of old industrial buildings – blast furnaces, power-hammers and suspension bridges. In the 1950s England invented the Industrial Archaelogy movement to safeguard mankind's industrial patrimony, as the nineteenth century safeguarded the medieval patrimony.

Eighteenth-century Christians could not imagine that medieval works might befit the glorification of God. Only eighteenth-century taste was worthy of this sacred role. And, in the name of the taste of the day, appalling vandalism was allowed to take place. The eighteenth century saw itself as having the monopoly of 'good taste'; medieval 'bad taste', or Gothic as it was then called, deserved only the demolition man's hammer.

In the abbey of Saint-Denis, in order to widen the doorways and make it easier for the dais to go in and out on ceremonial occasions, the pier was removed from the central doorway and the stone statue of St Denis broken. At the same time the lintels of the three portals and the carved columns representing the Old Testament kings and queens, which decorated the embrasures, were destroyed. Without hesitation, venerable old tombstones were ripped out of the floor in the choir and the glazed tiles were replaced by black and white paving stones. The prior, Dom Malaret, who was responsible for these misdoings, had no intention of stopping once he had set out on so worthy a path; he planned to remove the tombs of the Kings of France, which he found hideous and cumbersome, from their place in the transept and pile them in two chapels in the crypt. Only the state of the royal finances prevented him from carrying this out. From 1781 to 1784 Dom Malaret employed an Italian, Borani, to whitewash the whole interior of the church, a job which Borani had already carried out very conscientiously at Tours, Angers and Chartres.

So as to build a new high altar in the choir at Notre-Dame de Paris, Mansart, the famous architect of the Place Vendôme and of the Invalides, destroyed in 1699 the thirteenth-century high altar, the rood screen, the choir stalls, and the bas-reliefs on the inner enclosure of the ambulatory. The recumbent statues and mourning figures on old copper or stone tombs came to the same end. The columns in the apse were covered with marble slabs ornamented with gilded metal. Several years later workmen were employed to smash the thirteenth-century stained-glass windows and so in 1752 hammers shattered these great windows in the choir and they were replaced by plain glass with a border of *fleurs de lis*. In 1771, Soufflot, the architect of the Pantheon, broke the Almighty God who rose in majesty on the pier of the central door, he destroyed the wise and foolish virgins on either side of the door and, in the tympanum, the Resurrection of the Dead and the Archangel Michael holding the scales at the Last Judgement. All these sculptures have now been remade, but it is easy to tell from a thin line of cement which parts of the tympanum have been restored. Like Saint-Denis and many other churches of that period, the interior of Notre-Dame was whitewashed.

When Louis-André de Grimaldi, one of the princes of Monaco and Bishop of Le Mans, left that bishopric in 1777 for Noyon, the chapter, wishing to thank him for his 'improvements' to the cathedral, hung a portrait of him in the vestry with a eulogistic inscription in marble and the date 1778. In fact, during his episcopate, the thirteenth-century high altar, 'a confused heap of ornaments and copper', as well as the altars in the nave, in the transept, and in the side aisles, all disappeared. With the remains of the rood screen two eighteenth-century altars were made, and eight large pillars in the apse were covered in

Two of the rare stonecutters' marks to be seen at Saint-Denis.

marble stucco; 18,000–20,000 lb. of copperwork were sold. An antiquarian of the day, Chappotin de Saint-Laurent, tried in vain to prevent the chapter from carrying out this act of vandalism. He was not even given permission to copy out the old inscriptions on these objects. Thus an immense quantity of treasure was lost for ever.

The thirteenth-century high altars were replaced by eighteenth-century ones which can often still be seen in cathedral choirs like Notre-Dame de Paris or Notre-Dame de Chartres. The rood screens were replaced by wrought-iron railings and medieval chalices, monstrances and crosses made way for eighteenth-century ones. The extraordinary fact of the matter is that the men responsible were undeniably motivated by deep religious beliefs. Bishops, canons and private individuals sacrificed part of their fortunes in order to finance the changes which often cost astronomical sums. It must be said that this passion for redecoration and rebuilding is, in some ways, reminiscent of the twelfth- and thirteenth-century 'cathedral crusade'.

Bearing in mind this destruction carried out in the name of 'taste', we may ask ourselves whether modern Western society makes the same colossal mistakes when it speaks of 'good' and 'bad' taste as the eighteenth century did when referring with such arrogant assurance to *petit goût* and *grand goût*. There is little doubt that if a twentieth-century aesthete were suddenly carried back to the twelfth century to stand before the façade of Saint-Denis, where every sculpture was painted in violent, if not clashing, colours, he would exclaim in horror: 'What bad taste!'

To avoid such disappointment, the twentieth century has decided, when restoring these monuments, to leave the stone bare. But there can be no doubt that this is a betrayal of the Cluniac idea, of Suger's concept and of the cathedral builders themselves.

The Creative Impulse

It is hardly necessary to observe that medieval faith was the real point of departure for the 'cathedral crusade' whose evolution we shall outline. We shall see that circumstances were particularly favourable for the development of architectural expressions of piety. But it goes without saying that, had the Middle Ages not been a time of piety, the genius of the builders and the merchants' money would have been spent otherwise. We would have neither Chartres, nor Amiens, nor Strasbourg . . . Equally, although Suger's pride and the bourgeois vanity of the day are to be given proper prominence, the reader should not overlook the spiritual background against which they were played out, for these psychological elements were as important in their way as the economical and technical events with which we shall be dealing.

This is not the place to attempt more than a cursory mention of this background. Indeed, many works, from the beginning of the Romantic period to today, have presented a richly detailed picture of it. It could be dealt with more specifically, and certain adjustments could be made, but only within the context of a much wider study, which would particularly embrace theology and philosophy. There is one point concerning religion to which the reader's attention should especially be drawn, and this is the growth in the Marian cult which took place during the Middle Ages and which was to have a considerable effect on the building of cathedrals. St Bernard, who was really a central figure in the history of medieval Christianity, contributed enormously to the growth of the cult of the Virgin, which was celebrated at the time in liturgical hymns:

> O Salutary Virgin – Star of the Sea,
> Thou who bore the Sun of Justice;
> Creator of light, ever Virgin,
> Receive our praise.
> Queen of Heaven through whom the sick are cured,
> The faithful receive grace,
> The afflicted joy, and the world celestial light and
> Hope of salvation,
> Royal heart, Pure Virgin,
> Grant us thy care and protection,
> Receive our vows and by your prayers
> Save us from suffering!

The vaults of the transept of Amiens
(thirteenth century).

The Virgin Mary was most honoured and venerated at Notre-Dame de Chartres. According to tradition, a hundred years before the birth of Christ, there was a grotto on the very spot where the cathedral stands, where a virgin mother was worshipped in secret. Certain relics, supposedly belonging to the Virgin Mary, were piously preserved at Chartres : among others was the dress which she was said to have worn at the birth of Christ. This precious relic was miraculously saved from a fire in 1194, as was a piece of stained glass with a blue background – the same blue could not be found in the thirteenth century. This work, now known as Notre-Dame de Belle Verrière, was enshrined in a window in the choir in the thirteenth century.

In Notre-Dame de Senlis the life of the Virgin Mary ornaments the central portal, and in Notre-Dame de Paris two doorways were decorated with representations of the Virgin. At Rheims the pier of the central doorway has a statue of Our Lady. The Cistercian order placed its churches specifically under the Virgin Mary's protection, and during the twelfth century most of the great churches were dedicated to Our Lady: Notre-Dame de Laon, Notre-Dame d'Amiens, Notre-Dame de Paris.

The enthusiasm for cathedral building began in the second half of the twelfth century – at Sens in 1133, at Noyon in 1151, at Laon in 1160, at Notre-Dame de Paris in 1163 – and reached its high peak during the last part of the century and the first thirty years of so of the following century – at Bourges in 1192, at Chartres in 1194, at Rouen in 1202, at Rheims in 1211, at Le Mans in 1217, at Amiens in 1221 and at Beauvais, where the building was planned in 1225, but which was only begun in 1247. It has been noticed that these great cathedrals form, as it were, a crown around Notre-Dame de Paris – they go from Rheims in the east to Le Mans in the west and from Laon and Amiens in the north to Bourges in the south.

This enthusiasm lasted for another third of a century, long enough for the large part of these buildings to be well under way; then the passion for rebuilding gradually abated and work continued, although less actively, throughout the last years of the century and the first decades of the fourteenth century. The Hundred Years' War, which broke out to all intents and purposes in 1337, finally put an end to the building. Despite efforts made at the end of the Hundred Years' War (1453) and during the sixteenth century, no French cathedral was ever completely finished.

The cathedral towns are also bishops' seats. It was in about the fifth century that the Church decided which Gallo-Roman cities were to have bishops. Most of the episcopal cities were situated to the south of the Massif Central, in the parts of Gaul which were then most economically advanced and where the population was certainly denser than in the rest of the country. So Grasse, Vence and Antibes had bishops, as did Riez and Senez, towns whose names we no longer even know and which are on the borders of the Alpes-de-Haute-

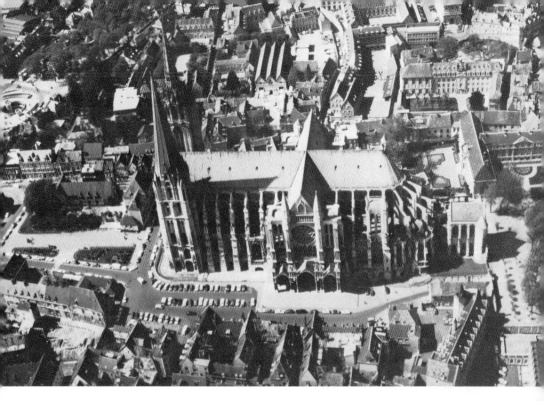

A cathedral surrounded by the town: Chartres.

Provence, one of the most deprived and underpopulated departments in France. Later, at the height of the Middle Ages, other parts of Ancient Gaul developed spiritually and economically, The towns mentioned above, which were episcopal cities during this period of ascendant Christianity, were not rich enough to build large cathedrals.

In most people's minds, the word 'cathedral' conjures up the idea of a large church, but, in fact, many cathedrals were built along modest lines. On the other hand, simple parish churches situated in prosperous areas were ambitiously conceived and they were bigger than many cathedrals. The history of cathedral building and the builders is closely linked to the regeneration of cities and commerce, to the birth of the bourgeoisie and the first civic liberties.

Exchanges between East and West were considerably hampered by the Arab invasion of the seventh century, as a result of which Western European trade and industry, which had managed to survive the barbarian invasions, came almost totally to a standstill. Urban life died away, there were practically no more merchants and municipal organization ceased to exist. The technical knowledge of antiquity was blurred in the mists of time. Had men mysteriously retained the secrets of stonemasonry, several centuries of groping around would not have been needed before a suitable technique of stonecutting was found.

Towns in the true sense of the word no longer existed, but only fortified castles. Europe became an agricultural continent where land was the only source of wealth. Western economy was an economy without trade and national revenue reached its lowest point. Then, in the tenth century, there was relative calm – vagabonds, rootless people, men in search of adventure or wanting to make money began to transport merchandise from one part of Europe to another and thus to revive trade. These men settled where two rivers met or where two important routes crossed.

Thanks to them and their activities, towns began to come into being again. Wise landowners attracted some of these dynamic groups and encouraged them to found towns. Henri Pirenne, the great Belgian medievalist, was struck by the parallel to be drawn between eleventh- and twelfth-century Europe and the American West in the nineteenth century. Even down to the finest details the resemblance between the eleventh- and twelfth-century 'new towns' and the towns laid out along the railway line by American entrepreneurs is in fact striking. Both were trying to attract settlers by favourable material and personal conditions; both had recourse to publicity. When a new town was to be built, its charter was proclaimed throughout the land – just as nowadays the press might issue the most wonderful prospectus.

In 1956 the author lectured in the United States, at Yale, on the similarities between French medieval evolution and the evolution of the United States. Thus he compared Beauvais to the Empire State Building, the Cistercians to Henry Ford, faith to liberty, La Beauce to the Great Plains and the gold *écu* to the dollar. To say, as he did, that American society was no longer a young society, that it was already at the height of its maturity, was quite simply to blaspheme. To forecast that this great country would begin to decline in the seventies and that its amazing technology would be partly outdated and the dollar devalued was at the time an incredible assertion.

As in the United States, the medieval economy developed through free enterprise and the right to work. The value of property increased greatly, limited companies were founded, and the expansion of the economy brought with it money-changers, bankers and industrialists. These were made to feel guilty by the Church, which was opposed to the idea of profit. So as to be forgiven, they had to give or bequeath part of their fortune to charitable works, such as the building of churches. In this way a powerful method of financing cathedrals was established. The greater the fortune amassed, the more willingly gifts were given.

From the start, the way of life in towns contrasted with that of the country dweller. The laws of an agricultural society could not apply to the new commercial life. Those who wished to establish a municipal and juridical

Laon: the cathedral and its medieval surroundings.

organization had often to struggle, even to fight; and this gave rise to the commune, a sworn society sanctioned by a charter. The oldest of these to the north of the Alps is Cambrai, which dates from 1077. The movement spread to towns like Sens, Noyon, Senlis, Laon, Rouen, Rheims, Amiens and Beauvais. Some towns like Paris become free towns (that is to say free of municipal taxation). Great cathedrals stand in all these cities.

There was, as has been pointed out, a fairly strong connection between the commercial strength of a city, its civic independence and the building of large churches. Nearly all the towns which acquired independence were situated on an important trade route, either a land route or by a river. In the Massif Central, which is a rather difficult part of the country to cross, there were very few communes and practically no large cathedrals. The same can be said of Brittany, which is off the beaten track and where there were no twelfth- or thirteenth-century communes or big churches.

In England the burghers were rarely able to obtain independence for their cities, and so the great churches were usually built without their active support. Besides which, a large number of episcopal churches are also monastic – the cathedrals at Durham, Canterbury and Gloucester, for instance, were built surrounded by monastic buildings which cut them off from the town.

The spirit of the medieval bourgeois played a decisive part in the 'cathedral crusade'. These men were inspired by fanatical local patriotism. It was a matter of pride to have taken away the feudal landlord's rights and the city's churches bore witness to the subsequent rejoicing. Nothing was too splendid or too big. The city was the bourgeois' country and he wanted outsiders to be impressed by the magnificence of the churches.

The enthusiasm of a young people is often expressed through the colossal and the immoderate. It was a youthful Egypt which erected the Great Pyramid during the first dynasties; it was the youthful United States which attempted to beat world records and which built ever taller skyscrapers. Despite the building of the Sears tower in Chicago and the twin World Trade Center towers in New York, it was really the Empire State Building with its 102 floors which put an end to the race upwards that took place during the years immediately before the Second World War.

Young medieval society, symbolized by the bourgeoisie, was gripped by the 'world record' fever and built its naves closer and closer to heaven. In 1163 Notre-Dame de Paris held the world record with its vault 32.8 metres from the ground. Chartres overtook Notre-Dame de Paris in 1194 with 36.55 metres. The vault of Rheims reached 37.95 metres in 1212 and the one at Amiens 42.3 metres in 1221. This 'world record' fever was to make itself felt once more in 1225 with the plans for the choir of Beauvais, whose vault was 48 metres high. (This vault in fact collapsed in 1284.) But the Middle Ages matured, the bourgeoisie became less dynamic, the 'world record' fever died away. Saint-Urbain was built at

Right: The choir, Laon Cathedral

32

Overleaf: Two 'world records': Beauvais in the thirteenth century and the Empire State Building.

Above and top right: Stained-glass windows from Beauvais showing masons at work.

Troyes – it was built of glass and conceived in an entirely new spirit.

When the United States reached maturity in 1947 (the year when Truman's doctrine placed America at the head of the 'free nations') industrial circles gradually lost their dynamism and the 'world record' fever no longer gripped the people. In 1953 the famous Lever House Building was put up on Park Avenue, New York. It was a glass building with only thirty floors and it was put there not for financial reasons, but for aesthetic ones. In fact the aesthetic reasons tend, to a certain extent, to take over from business ones. This building symbolizes a psychological turning point in the evolution of the United States.

The merchants' conscience, the bourgeois' civic sense and the 'world record'

Chartres Cathedral: stonecutters at work.

fever may all have contributed to the success of the 'cathedral crusade' but other circumstances besides facilitated the financing of these buildings.

From the middle of the twelfth century, the idea of going to the Holy Land became less popular. Was it because Jerusalem had been in Christian hands since 1099? Was it because people did not appreciate the continual Muslim threat to the Frankish kingdoms? Was it because of memories of the First Crusade? Or had a taste for luxury and prosperity begun to take a hold? Whatever the case, the Church authorized those responsible for building to grant indulgences to those who helped to erect the house of God. A man need no longer go on a crusade to expiate his sins. The 'cathedral crusade' took shape and the whole hierarchy of the Church, from the Pope to the simple parish priest, took part both spiritually and financially. Thus, after the failure of the appallingly organized expeditions of 1147, 1187, and 1204, crusades to defend Christ's tomb became an idea of the past and the difficulties encountered by St Louis when he formed his army in the middle of the thirteenth century were characteristic of the spirit of the times. It could be said that the 'cathedral crusade', in establishing itself, contributed to the weakening of the Frankish kingdom.

Contrary to popular opinion, the 'cathedral crusade' met with considerable resistance. Pious men in important positions were profoundly shocked by these great works. Pierre le Chantre, a highly placed cathedral dignitary in Paris, wrote vehemently in 1180 : 'It is a sin to build the kind of churches which are being built nowadays.' 'This ever-present passion for building' he referred to as a 'sickness', an overwhelming epidemic. 'Monastic churches and cathedrals are being built by usury and avarice, by cunning and lies, and by the deception of preachers.'

But Pierre le Chantre had no more influence on the building of cathedrals than St Bernard had on the luxury of Cluny or Saint-Denis. The words above were dictated by wisdom, perhaps, but they were powerless against the zeal and the emotion which drove the builders on. The house of God was being built in the image of the Heavenly City, and this house of God was an admirable thing : it was the place of worship and the home of the people.

In most ancient religions, the people were not allowed into the Holy of Holies, the house of God. But the Christian Church invited the faithful to contribute to the cost of buildings which would be so vast that the crowds could enter the sanctuary. Ecclesiastic legislation distinguishes between the sanctuary and the rest of the cathedral. In the Middle Ages Notre-Dame de Paris belonged not to the bishop but to the chapter, but the chapter's jurisdiction did not include the sanctuary, which could belong only to the bishop. The nave and the side aisles were particularly reserved for worshippers – the people.

It is crucial to understand this distinction if the twentieth-century mind is not to be shocked by the lively activities which took place inside the churches. People ate and slept there, they talked without whispering. They could bring in

Top: Masons laying stones with level, stonecutters at work. Labourers with pulley basket and ladder; workmen on scaffolding. (Early twelfth-century French Bible.) *Bottom:* Master carpenter supervising workmen building a roof. (Fourteenth century, *Vie de Saint-Denis.*)

Top: Masons at work with trowel, labourers carrying stones (*Censier* of the Abbey of Sainte-Geneviève, Paris). *Bottom:* Mason with plumb line and set square; stonecutter with chisel and mallet; labourers mixing and carrying mortar. (Drawing: Herrade de Landsberg, *Hortus Deliciarum*, *1181–85*.)

their dogs or their sparrow-hawks. Since there were no pews it was of course easier to move about than it is nowadays. Matters not concerning religion were discussed there – representatives of the commune met there over municipal affairs; and it has been observed elsewhere that in some towns where communes were founded and large churches built there was no town hall.

There is a known text which forbids a certain commune to use the cathedral as a meeting-room. This shows that it was usual practice to do so. It was obviously not a right, but a habit generally tolerated by the Church. In Marseilles meetings of the city fathers, magistrates and the heads of guilds regularly took place in the Church of La Major. It may be supposed that the commune's representatives helped to finance the cathedral with, in the back of their minds, the idea of holding their meetings there. We may find this embarrassing but it must be understood that these men lived in daily contact with religion. At that time men were probably far less intimidated by Our Lord than today's believer who, at most, only confronts his God on Sunday morning in the parish church.

Equally, it must be realized that professional groups did not think they were behaving disrespectfully when they advertised themselves in the cathedral at Chartres. There was no evil thought behind it. On close inspection it can be seen that the professional groups acquired the very best positions in the church for their stained glass, which is in the side aisles or in the ambulatory, close to the public, whereas the windows given by bishops and noblemen are high up in the nave and the choir. In these stained-glass windows, the clothier, the stonecutter, the cartwright or the carpenter is represented at the bottom of the window, as near as possible to his prospective clients.

The very quantity of medieval feast days increased the contact men had with God and justified their passion for the rebuilding of churches. No civilization, it would appear, has ever given so many official holidays to peasants and workmen. It was not until February 1956 that France, by granting three weeks' annual holiday in addition to ten feast days, became the first country in the world to allow its citizens about as many days' holiday as were granted by the Church in the Middle Ages. It must be acknowledged, however, that in olden times a day's work was considerably longer than it is now. Work began, more often than not, at dawn and continued until sunset.

The number of feast days varied from town to town and from year to year. In addition to the fifty-two Sundays there were some thirty feast days. The builders' accounts confirm these facts. In the statement of accounts for the building of the Cistercian abbey at Vale Royal in England in 1280, twenty-nine feast days are enumerated. Holidays were not paid in those days, whereas today the law insists that certain days off be paid. Work stopped early on Saturday afternoon, just as it stopped around noon on the eve of feast days. If these half-holidays are added to the feast days, the medieval men worked for an average of only four or five days a week. This has been borne out by the detailed accounts of 1229 for the building of the Augustinian convent in Paris. Workmen engaged by the day were never paid for more than five days a week and were sometimes only paid for four.

The following are the expenses for the second week of August (12 deniers=1 sou, 20 sous=1 pound): to Maître Robert for five days – 10s.; to three masons for five days each – 29s. 2d.; to five assistants for five days each – 24s. 7d. For the third week of August : to Maître Robert for five days – 10s. And for the last week of August : to Maître Robert for four days – 8s.; to Jehan de Saint Quentin, to Girart de Van . . . to Guillaume, stonecutters, four days each at 2 sous a day, 24s. And finally, the expenses for the second week of September : to Maître Robert for five days – 10s.; to two assistants and a scaffolder for five days each – 15s. 10d.

These accounts speak for themselves. The medieval working populations was not overburdened and the workers were certainly not to be pitied. The feast days were magnificently organized by the authorities and everything was absolutely free. The splendour of medieval religious feast days is now almost beyond imagination; nowadays only the ceremonial at St Peter's in Rome begins to compare with it. The spare time in the Middle Ages must have had a considerable influence on the 'cathedral crusade' and on the enlargement of churches.

On great feast days, the ecclesiastic authorities had to concentrate their efforts on ceremonies in the cathedral at the expense of the parish churches. The people from different parishes wanted to attend the celebrations in the cathedral. It was not unlike the atmosphere today when an international match is to be played at an important stadium and the crowds from round about rush to see it, abandoning local matches in suburban sports grounds. The stadium where the international match is to be played has to be as large as possible. For comparable reasons – *mutatis mutandis* – the medieval cathedral had to be big enough to hold the people who came from every corner of the town; and so, because of the vast numbers of the faithful, the authorities had constantly to plan enlargements to cathedrals. Some of them had been made big enough to hold more people than there were inhabitants of the town, as the peasants from neighbouring parishes were also accounted for.

When the burgher and his wife came out of their dark house with its closed wooden shutters and made their way towards the celebrations through narrow, winding streets, the towers and spires of the cathedral seen across the roofs seemed to them even taller and slenderer than they do to us. The area of the town was limited by the city walls, and land inside the fortifications was expensive and sought after, so houses were built right up to the edge of the churches. There was hardly any empty space; and it was never possible in the Middle Ages to admire the whole cathedral from a certain distance, as we do today. The old houses around the cathedrals have now, as often as not, been

A fresco from Saint-Savin-sur-Gartempe showing the building of the Tower of Babel.

demolished. Notre-Dame de Paris has the most ill-proportioned square in front of it; Napoleon III, who feared that rioters in a possible revolution might be able to barricade themselves in the neighbouring narrow streets, had that part of the city razed. But whatever the immediate surroundings, we are lucky to be able to visit cathedrals without having to put up with the hurly-burly and noise of a vast building site. To his sorrow, the medieval townsman never saw his cathedral finished. He could only hope that his son would one day see an end to the apparently eternal chaos, with people of all trades busy in a limited space amongst wagons laden with building materials. There were sculptors, stonecutters, masons, plasterers, tilers, scaffolders, smiths, foremen, lead workers, stonefitters and many others. Scaffolding attached to the walls hid part of the building. If there was a compensation it was that, on seeing all this, the townsman of the day at least had the satisfaction of being able to supervise the judicious use of the money which he had contributed. Doubtless, too, he was encouraged to even further generosity. What seventeenth-century citizen would have given part of his fortune to please an absolute monarch?

The passer-by who approached the main doorway, in faith or out of curiosity, had the pleasure of recognizing characters from the Old and New Testaments – characters who were dear to his heart and soul. The fact that the educated man

Top: An architect with a set square and a foreman's compass (*Vie de Saint Offar,* thirteenth century). *Bottom:* Mason and stonecutter at work (*Grandes Chronique de France, c. 1379).*

and the people had the same terms of reference, the same picture book, at this time lent a certain harmony to the age. Everyone had received the same education, albeit to a different level. Centuries later things were to be otherwise when, as a result of the excessive cult of antiquity, the educated Renaissance man had scenes from mythology painted and sculpted which were quite incomprehensible to the people. The introduction of the classics separated the educated man from the people for several centuries. The breach has not yet been entirely closed in Western Europe to this day.

On going further into the church, the citizen would find other familiar scenes. Until about the middle of the twelfth century, the picture book continued to unfold – frescoes covered the walls and the vaulting at, for instance, Saint-Savin. Then, little by little, larger windows meant smaller walls and vast frescoes became an impossibility. Then the stained glass took over the role of picture book.

Men of every social condition gathered under the cathedral vault, and this was another aspect of medieval unity. The bourgeois, the peasant, the bishop, the nobleman, the prince and even the king met here. Great men went to pray in the cathedral and gave large sums to the church. The time had not yet come when rich believers devoted their fortunes to building luxurious private chapels.

This coming together of the faithful of all classes under the aegis of the Church was solemnly expressed, for all to see, in inscriptions on a circular paving stone in the middle of the nave which formed the centre of a labyrinth. Here could be found the names and portraits of those who had contributed to the building of the cathedral. Next to the bishop's portrait were portraits of the architects. The stones, laid in the pattern of a labyrinth, were thought to represent the pilgrim's path to the Holy Land. This symbolism was taken so seriously that, according to the beliefs of the time, the same grace and indulgences could be obtained from the labyrinth as from the pilgrimage itself. This may seem strange and it gave the builders an unexpected importance. But it must be remembered that architectural vocabulary has always played a large part in Christian symbolism; notable examples of this are the evangelical use of the word 'cornerstone', and the title of 'Pontiff' (builder of bridges), which was taken from the Romans.

Only three examples of these labyrinths survive to this day; they are at Chartres, Saint-Quentin and Guingamp. The origins of this type of layout must be found in Cretan civilizations, although it is equally possible that it was introduced to Western Europe in megalithic times, since there is, at the entrance to the Dublin Museum, a megalithic labyrinth engraved in stone.

The faithful piously worked their way through the maze on their knees until they reached the symbolic central stone. Unfortunately none of the original stones remain, but the inscriptions from Amiens and Rheims survive, as they were carefully copied and preserved. The one from Amiens reads: 'In the Year of Grace 1220, work was begun on this church. The bishop of this diocese was then

Site with pulleys, scaffolding and builders at work (*Grandes Chroniques de Saint-Denis*, fourteenth century)

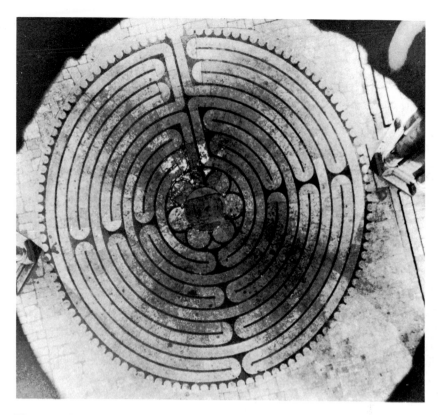

The stone labyrinth in the nave at Chartres.

Évrard; the King of France was Louis son of Philip the Wise. The master of the works was Maître Robert de Luzarches and after him came Thomas de Cormont and then the latter's son, Renaud, who had this inscription made in the Year of the Incarnation 1288.'

The portraits of the bishop and the three architects were inlaid in white marble. The highest dignitaries of the Church, the great feudal noblemen, the peasant and the bourgeois alike travelled on their knees through the labyrinth to find at its heart the names and faces of men of genius, men who were often of humble origin but who had dared to dream up this extraordinary architecture. These stones bear important witness against the theory of the anonymity of the cathedral builders. The honour of having your name engraved in the house of God was an encouragement and an inspiration, which the Church, in allowing these inscriptions, was wise to foster.

The Canon Builders

The primary importance of the chapter has to be appreciated before the building of a cathedral can be understood. Legend has told us of the part played by the bishop in the working out of plans and in the financing of the great enterprise, and certainly many cathedrals have a debt of gratitude to some of their bishops: Notre-Dame de Paris owes much to Maurice de Sully, Senlis to Thibaut and Amiens to the bishop Geoffroy d'Eu. But the legend should not mislead us – the bishop only occasionally played a part.

The bishop was a star who shone but then disappeared from the scene, and yet work on the cathedral continued from one generation to the next. Thanks to whom? Who, if not the chapter, looked after the cathedral? Besides, we know that sometimes the cathedral belonged not to the bishop but to the chapter. Hugues de Bourgogne gave the land on which the cathedral at Autun was built to the chapter rather than to the bishop.

The meaning of the word 'chapter' should first of all be clarified, as it no longer has the same meaning it had in the Middle Ages. Since the Revolution, in France the role of the chapter has been more honorary than active. In the Middle Ages it was a gathering of canons who enjoyed great privileges, and who were often outside episcopal jurisdiction. Their position *vis-à-vis* the bishop was only defined in the sixteenth century by the Council of Trent. But in England the privileges of the chapter are the same as they were in the Middle Ages. On a television programme about the 900th anniversary of the foundation of Winchester Cathedral, the bishop publicly recognized that the chapter was not within his jurisdiction. In fact, in order to enter the cathedral cloister by a certain 'secret' door, the bishop himself had to ask the chapter for the key.

The title of 'cathedral builders' should go to the canons; it is to them that the honour is due. They directed and masterminded the 'cathedral crusade' and continued the work over the centuries, often at their own expense, long after the general enthusiasm had died down. We should look, then, at the historical origins of the chapter and how it managed to play so important a part in the temporal legislation of the Church.

During the 1970s York Minster was in danger of collapsing. The rebuilding of the entire foundations was undertaken with the help of the most advanced technology and thanks to a budget of several million pounds.

Left and right: Thirteenth-century Canterbury Psalter.

In the early Middle Ages the bishop had a body of priests who helped him to administer the diocese and to say mass in the parishes. The Bishop of Metz, Chrodegang (742–66), is said to have instituted the canonical system in order to regulate the lives of these priests. These priests or canons, who to a certain extent were the bishop's privy councillors, were obliged to lead a community life. They had, from that time, to sleep in dormitories, eat in a refectory and celebrate their office together.

In 817, at Aix-la-Chapelle, Louis the Pious confirmed that canons should take a vow of obedience and chastity, but more or less annulled the vow of poverty. This was to have important consequences. Canons were allowed to have rights over their real estate for life and to dispose of their chattels by a will. This decision meant that the canons gradually withdrew from the community and returned to a more private and secular way of life.

From the first half of the tenth century, several cathedral chapters were allowed to separate their incomes from the bishop's. From then on the chapter's independence grew. The chapter now had a common fund at its disposal and a considerable income or prebend went with each canonry. This income did not always oblige the canon to live in the cathedral town itself and some canons were

even able to claim several prebends from different dioceses, there being resident and non-resident canons. The establishment of a dean at the head of the chapter added to its independence.

The chapter also included a certain number of dignitaries; there were, for instance, a chancellor, who acted as secretary and who was in charge of seals, a treasurer responsible for the treasure and the relics, and a cantor, who was the choirmaster and whose job it was to organize religious services. In episcopal protocol, canons took precedence over mitred abbots.

The growth of towns and a larger population meant more canons. The development of trade and the profitable use of agricultural land increased the value of the prebends and, by extension, the power of the chapters. Little by little the canons added to their rights and privileges and became protective of their authority, even to the extent of trying to limit the power of the bishop. Quarrels about jurisdiction became more and more common, and they were usually resolved to the advantage of the powerful canons, as was the case at Notre-Dame de Paris in 1335. As the result of an incident, the bishop himself was forced to recognize, in the act of 5 November 1335, that the dean and chapter – in particular each canon ('the members of the choir of Notre-Dame and all their attendants') – were exempt from his jurisdiction, and he had to repudiate his legal advisers if they had said the opposite.

In all cathedrals the chapter was in charge of the fabric and the works, which meant, in the Middle Ages, everything concerning the building and upkeep of the church, both in practical matters and in the raising and administration of the necessary funds. The bishop never seems to have been expected to contribute to building costs; whenever he did, it was of his own free will and as an exception.

In the drawing up of plans and the carrying out of works, the chapter's role was comparable to that of a present-day director of urban redevelopment. The same kind of problems had to be solved: compulsory purchasing, financing, adjudication and other difficulties not unlike those encountered today. When personal and public interest are brought into conflict, compulsory purchase, in particular, has always been a source of bitter contention, and the obstinacy of one religious community in the thirteenth century presented the cathedral builders in Amiens with a case in point. Between 1230 and 1240 the friars of the Hôtel-Dieu in Amiens refused to see that, in the interests of the town, the cathedral needed enlarging, albeit at the expense of the neighbouring Hôtel-Dieu. Their bad faith was such that vast indemnities had to be granted to gain their consent and their hospital had to be rebuilt by the chapter near a large waterway. They were given a hundred pounds a year for five years and an impartial commission of four was nominated to assess the cost of their moving. Measures also had to be taken to avoid dreadful brawls between the friars who wanted to go and those who preferred to stay. It took a long time to persuade the latter they they had to submit to the will of the people and the clergy. Twentieth-century villagers might well invoke these thirteenth-century ecclesiastics.

The canons met together, in principle, once a year to appoint an overseer who would be the fabric and works accountant and also director of the site. This post might be filled by a canon or a clergyman, or, more exceptionally, by a layman responsible to the chapter. He was chosen for his knowledge of architecture and his business acumen.

We are fortunate in having the detailed accounts for the fabric of the cathedral at Autun for the year 1294-5, a simple document worth much other literature as it reveals innumerable fascinating details about the activities on a thirteenth-century cathedral site. Quicherat studied it in the nineteenth century, since when few scholars have paid any attention to it.

In the year 1295 on the Friday after the octave of Pentecost, Robert Clavel, clerk and overseer for the chapter of the Church of Saint-Lazare, did the accounts for all expenses and receipts made in the name of the said chapter since the Monday after the octave of Pentecost 1294 until the Sunday in the octave of Pentecost of the afore-mentioned year, 1295, and having subtracted 12 pounds and 11

Construction of the Temple: Bible of
Saint-Pierre de Rodas (twelfth century).

gabihele angtm in eade uisionen
iuxta peesewsde uniuersa ept com
pleta dedux· Nun morrente sup
ducto rege medou· & succedente
in regno cyro rege psaru pmissi
onem di copletam peunde regem
pplorum hirtm reducto storia sedi
libus patali pomenon· & inucu essez
pphe cofirmat· Cunq· appo ist
& seniozib templu di aedificare coe
pissent· mozuo cyrorege hac recu
nante rege psaru quinemorito
successerit uicine gentis cuutatis
hirtm ut hiisde eldras refert· restau
racionem tepli & cuutatis resistedo
impedire coeper· Qua racione de
terra ppl isrt reparacio sup dict
templi dni· nec dn iuxta pmissione
cocessam eez· ist psi qd insede amorai
nu memorati dari regis ysrru· Ag
geus ppha ado missis et· Zorobas
bel de tribu erat uida qui potestati
regis susceu uisent· & ihesu siliu
iosedech sumu saedote· admona ut
credulu copleto annou· numero
tepi restauracionis hirtm aduenu
se· hoceia addito de incredulitate
ppli uolut monitari & quod dspeuu
dixera· ipsi hic die· nun du uena temp
ut aedificet dom di· Omia au queru
tum hui ppha conteet· reuersione
ppli aedificacione templi renoua
cione cuutatis obseruanciam saedo
talem· & interitu regiou gencu
exterru siguisicat·   tdluc

egis in mse sexto
idie una mensis
ctu e uerbu dni in
anu aggei pphe ad
robabel siliu sala
l duce uida· & ad
um siliu iosedech
aedote magnu di
ens· Haec du dns
cercituu dics· Psts
du· Nodu uenit
mp dom dnu aedi
icande· & sactu
t uerbu dni in ma
u aggei pphe di
uf· Numquid tep
uob ut habiteus
omub laqueatis· &
us ista deserta·
ue hec du dns exercituu
ce corda ura sup uias uras·
minas tis multu· & intulistis
paruu· Comedistis· & n estis sa
ciati· bibistis· & n estis inhebria
ti· Operuistis uos· & n estis cale
facti· & qui mercedes cogregu
uit· misit eas insacculu ptusu
aec du dns exercituu· Ponite cor
da ura sup uias uras· ascendi
te inmonte· poirate lignu· &
aedisicate domu· & acceptabilis
muherit· & glousicabor du dns·
R espexistis ad amplius· & ecce sa
tu e min· & intulistis indomu
& exsusslaui illud· Qua ob cau
sam du dns exercituu· quia do
mus mea deserta e· & uos sesti
nastis unus quisq· indomu sua·
p hoc sup uos pibiti scaeli ne
darent rore· & tra pibiti est
ne dara germi siu· & uocaui
siccitate sup tra· & sup montes
& sup trmcu· & sup uinu· & sup
oleu· & que cuq· psert humus·
& sup homines· & sup umta·
& sup omne labore manuum·

deniers as a tithe and not forgetting to deduct the advances received with these expenses in view, it remains that the chapter at Autun owes the said Robert 53 pounds, 6 sous, 3 Viennese deniers, a sum which the said Robert owed the chapter at Autun according to the account done on the said Monday.

Quicherat analysed Robert Clavel's receipts and found that seven items made up the entire income.

1.Taxes levied on the chapter at Autun.

2.Income from vacant benefices in the city and diocese of Autun which, by the authority of the Holy See, has been assigned to the cathedral works.

3.Income from indulgences granted to benefactors to the fabric.

4.Income from the collection and from the Saint-Lazare brotherhood at the Pentecostal synod.

5.Casual offerings: this item includes sums not accounted for by the works fund. They amounted to 34 pounds, 19 sous, 5 deniers. Included are several bequests made by individuals from other dioceses, among them one from a woman in Cluny; but, generally speaking, donations came from the diocese of Autun, from peasants, except in the case of one Magister Humbertus de Virgultis, whose name indicates that he was a clerk. The parish priests of Buxy and Saffres brought, on the one hand, 5 sous and 9 deniers, and on the other 14 sous towards the hire of carts in the parish. The village of Marcheseuil, which belonged to the chapter, provided 12 sous and 2 deniers in the same way.

6.Income from collection boxes specifically designated for the fabric (from Isabelle Raclete, the curé of Autun, Martinet the draper, Grimoard, Robin the goldsmith and casemaker, Gilles Gododin at Saint-Pancrace d'Autun, from Saint-Jean de la Crotte and from the church at Bligny), in all 10 pounds, 17 sous 2 deniers.

7.Additional item including 42 pounds, 13 sous, 3 deniers deducted from the collections at Autun Cathedral between Whitsun 1294 and Whitsun 1295.

The total income set forth, not including the last item, comes to 400 pounds, 9 sous and 9 deniers; and the expenses were as follows:

To the quarries for the excavation of stone destined to the upkeep of Saint-Lazare, 8 pounds, 10 sous, 4 deniers.

To the same for a year's supply of lime, 9 pounds, 8 sous.

For the cutting and transportation of cask wood for the vaulting in the church of Saint-Lazare, to the carpenters and labourers, 17 pounds, 2 sous, 7 deniers.

To the forge at Autun for the year, 42 pounds, 10 sous, 6 deniers.

To the quarry forge 62 sous, including our iron, 3 pounds, 2 sous.

To the labourers for opening the said quarry, 4 pounds, 15 sous, 4 deniers.

For investigations into the situation of the quarry at Marmontain, 1 pound 10 sous.

To the labourers who laid the tiles on the roof of the church of Saint-Lazare, 1 pound, 9 sous, 11 deniers.

For the poles for rafters, 5 sous.

For the making of 12 carts including the ironwork, 1 pound, 15 sous.

To the carpenters for the cask wood cut in the chapter's forest, 8 pounds, 16 sous.

For repairing the roof of the church of Saint-Lazare and the replacing of the necessary machinery, 3 pounds, 15 sous.

To the carpenters for lathing at the church of Saint-Lazare, 10 pounds, 8 sous.

To the cost of the lathing, 3 sous, 6 deniers.

For nails and other iron pieces necessary to building the sanctuary of the church of Saint-Lazare, 16 sous, 8 deniers.

To Master Pierre de Dijon, roofer, 70 pounds.

To the same, the said Pierre had 12 pounds accounted for on the previous account.

For expenses involved in moving the stones called gargoyles, 4 pounds, 10 sous, 9 deniers.

To Renaud, the innkeeper, for the rent of a house for the present aforementioned master for two terms of the current year, 3 pounds.

For clothing for the said master, not including the coming term of the birth of St John the Baptist, 10 pounds.

For iron pegs and for iron, 18 sous, 3 deniers.

For making the roofers' hammers, 1 sou, 10 deniers.

To the saddler, Benoît, for saddles, yokes, halters and other leather articles needed for the carts, 2 pounds, 10 sous.

For hay and harnessing, 19 pounds, 17 sous, 4 deniers.

For oats, 25 pounds, 3 sous, 9 deniers.

For shoeing the horses, 4 pounds, 6 sous.

For iron and nails used in making the carts and to repair the old ones, 6 pounds, 9 sous, 1 denier.

To the cartwright for the new carts and for repairs to the old ones, 2 pounds, 14 sous, 9 deniers.

For the tallow, the oil, the vinegar and 30 pounds of candles for the year, 2 pounds, 7 sous.

For the hire and expenses of the cart, 18 pounds.

For the hire of sheds, stables and granaries, 2 pounds.

For rope, 13 deniers.

For treatment to a horse, 5 sous.

For a horse to pull the cart, 3 pounds, 10 sous.

An overseer like Robert Clavel had not only to provide the working site with raw materials and manufactured goods, and see to the transport of these goods, but had also to organize the workmen, to make sure that religious services could continue despite the work and to arrange for the maintenance of completed building work. In 1295 Robert Clavel managed to balance his account, but often the expenses outran the chapter's resources, the basic income being insufficient for the cost of materials and labour. Then the men would leave the town and go to work on another site.

Generally speaking, the workmen in the Middle Ages feared neither canons nor kings. Among the accounts for Westminster Abbey there is an edict dated 25 November 1252 and promulgated by Henry III, one of the few monarchs to have financed a great church. According to this edict, it was essential to raise money urgently in order to tempt the workmen back to the site: 'Philip Lovel, treasurer, and Edward of Westminster (Master of the Works) are ordered by means of funds from the royal treasury and other moneys owed to the King, to recall to the church at Westminster workmen who, the King has been informed, have left, so that work may continue speedily . . .'

In similar cases the canons strove to discover new methods of raising money so that work could continue. They told confessors to remind the faithful that all money acquired by bad means should be given to the fabric. Young religious fraternities which had been founded to help fabrics like Saint-Lazare at Autun were urged to greater efforts in organizing their collections. Clerics who arrived late for church were fined. From the pulpit, preachers reminded their flock of the spiritual grace granted to benefactors of the cathedral. 'Beautiful and gentle people,' said a preacher in Amiens in 1260, 'you can be twenty-seven days nearer to Paradise than you were yesterday, unless you lose this indulgence through sin, envy and lust, and so can you advance the souls of your fathers, your mothers and all those whom you wish to include.' In addition, the chapter decided that people who wanted to be buried within the precincts of the cathedral had to pay a certain sum of money. Finally, when the need was felt, the canons would tax themselves more heavily. It must also be recognized that in difficult times bishops gave considerable sums to the fabric.

One of the most successful ways of collecting money was by organizing for relics to go on tour. The churches which owned important and famous relics were fortunate.

In 1112 at Laon, three months after fire had ravaged the cathedral, seven canons and some laymen set out with the relics which had been saved from the flames – a fragment of the Virgin Mary's gown, part of the sponge of the Passion and a piece of the true Cross. They visited in turn Issoudun, Tours, Angers, Le Mans and Chartres and they came home in the autumn with what they hoped would be enough money to rebuild their cathedral. However, these funds were quickly spent and in the spring of 1113 it was decided that a second tour should be arranged – this time overseas. They would go to England. So the canons made their way to Arras and Saint-Omer and reached the sea at Wissant. The crossing

Fourteenth-century illustrated Bible (*Grandes Chroniques de France,*
c. 1379).

was far from peaceful. The pious travellers were robbed by Flemish cloth
merchants and attacked by pirates. Nevertheless, they arrived intact at Dover
and went on to visit Canterbury, Winchester, Salisbury and Exeter. They
returned with enough money for the church to be consecrated on 29 August
1114.

But the cult of relics led to abuses. Relics of doubtful authenticity were
displayed, and as a result of these excesses the Church acted and, at the Lateran
Council in 1215, forbade the veneration of any object unless specific permission
were granted. From then onwards the cult of relics lost its intensity and in the
accounts of, for instance, Autun there is no further mention of sums raised by
these means. Abuses, however, continued. Tales of the day and, a little later,
Boccaccio's short stories abounded in indignant mockery directed at various
stratagems which barely differed from simple fraud. This indignation turned to
open revolt and was eventually to become one of the causes of the Reformation.

Working the Stone

In the hierarchy of cathedral builders the labourer is clearly at the bottom of the ladder, but, so long as the Middle Ages were in the ascendant, he had every opportunity to better himself. By his work and his intelligence he could become a specialized craftsman; he could save a little money and set himself up on his own as a contractor, or he could study to become an architect. Medieval society allowed the humblest of men to fill the highest offices. The future belonged to the ambitious. There is a certain analogy to be drawn between the evolution of the medieval worker's world and the evolution of the American worker's world. The medieval labourer could, so to speak, become a self-made man and acquire a respected position in the town.

Labourers were mainly recruited from among the rootless, often serfs fleeing from their feudal lords who came to find shelter in towns far away from their birthplaces. If they were not found by their masters before a year and a day were up, they became freemen and citizens of the town. Labourers also came from peasant families with large numbers of children, some of whom left home in search of freedom and adventure in the towns. They could find immediate employment in any of the numerous workshops in the town. Workers on the sites were free men.

The work given to the labourers varied. Records at Autun show they helped the carpenters to transport the cask wood, they dug to open up quarries and took tiles to the roof of the church of Saint-Lazare. Accounts from the Augustinian convent in Paris show that, among other tasks, they dug the foundations. There are frequent entries like: 'For removal of earth in order to build foundations. To Gautier for removing earth for the foundations of the sacristy. To Gautier for clearing the foundations.'

On the sites they carried a variety of materials in baskets on their backs, as can be seen from the following extracts: 'To two pannier bearers, three days each, 3 sous, 6 deniers. To seven pannier bearers, five days each, 20 sous, 5 deniers.' The daily wage for these labourers was about 7 deniers; semi-skilled workers like plasterers earned 10 or 11 deniers and specialized workmen like masons and stonecutters were paid about 20 or 22 deniers. Living conditions for labourers

Reinforced concrete in the foundations of
York Minster.

must, therefore, have been quite hard, as the wages were not very high and, above all, work was intermittent.

It is hard to reconcile the presence of these labourers on the site with the legend of voluntary work. This can only have been episodic and can have accounted for only a tiny part of the construction force. The unpaid workman was in effect taking the bread from the mouths of men in search of work. The only jobs which could be done by an unskilled labourer were carrying and digging, and labourers must have looked askance at anyone who offered his services free of charge.

The *chanson de geste* about the four Aymon sons tells the story of a legendary nobleman, Renaud de Montauban, who, in expiation of his sins, went to work on a site. He accepted only the humblest wage. After a week the workmen began to worry and joined forces against this man who was ruining prices; they decided to kill him and hit him on the head from behind with a hammer and threw his body in the Rhine. The crime did not go unpunished as, luckily, the fish gathered themselves together and lifted up the body which travelled down the current lit by three candles. This story symbolizes the workers' hostility towards the unpaid labour of the zealously faithful.

Specialized workers like stonecutters and masons had a certain number of labourers to help them at their jobs. These were called servants or assistants. The accounts quoted above are informative on this subject: 'To five stonecutters, 2 pounds, 10 sous. To four servants, 19 sous. To three masons, five days each, 1 pound, 9 sous, 2 deniers. To five assistants, five days each, 1 pound, 4 sous, 7 deniers.' Some of these labourers specialized in the making of mortar and plaster: 'To two plasterers' assistants, four days each, 8 sous. To four valets for sifting sand and making cement, three days each, 7 sous, 4 deniers.' Other accounts referred to these men as plasterers. It should be noted in passing that too much attention should not be paid to the names given to different workmen, since precision of words or indeed of figures did not have the importance it has today.

In the middle of the thirteenth century, masters of guilds were concerned with the moral and professional qualifications of labourers, who attained a relative degree of specialization. In 1268 the Provost of Merchants, Étienne Boileau, perhaps on the advice of St Louis, called the masters of the guilds to the Châtelet and asked them to dictate the 'usages and customs' of their professions. In this way Étienne Boileau registered 101 trades. The forty-eighth statute, which concerns us here, refers to 'masons, stonecutters and plasterers', and must have been dictated by Guillaume de Saint-Patu, the King's master mason. The King made his own architect master of the guild: 'The King, God grant him a good life, has given the mastership of the masons to Master Guillaume de Saint-Patu for as long as it pleases him. The said Master Guillaume swore in the palace lodge in Paris to watch loyally and honestly over the said craft, as well for the poor as for

A stonecutter at work to restore the south doorway at Saint-Denis. The lodge on the site continues a very old tradition.

the rich, for the weak as for the strong, so long as it shall please the King to give him charge of this craft. Then this Master Guillaume made the same oath to the Provost of Paris at the Châtelet.'

The guild master took advantage of such an occasion to safeguard his privileges: 'The master who looks after the craft for the King is exempt from keeping the watch in return for the services he renders in looking after the craft.' Paragraph four states that the master alone is allowed two apprentices instead of one. This statute, like others from the *Livre des Métiers*, combats fraudulence and attempts to guarantee quality in the building. 'If plasterers send plaster for the use of any man, the mason who works for this man to whom the plaster is sent must be careful, on his oath, that the measure of plaster is good and true and if he has any doubts about the measure, he must weigh it himself or have it weighed in front of him, and if he finds that the measure is false, the plasterer must pay a fine of 5 sous, that is to say 2 sous to the chapel of Saint-Blaise, 2 sous to the guild master and 1 sou to the man who has measured the plaster.'

The guild master did not forget himself. The following paragraph states that only the plasterer had to pay an entrance fee to his guild in Paris. 'No one can be a plasterer in Paris unless he pays 5 Parisian sous to the master who keeps the guild for the King. When he has paid the 5 sous, he must swear by the saints that he will put nothing except lime in the plaster and that he will deliver a true and honest measure.' Paragraph XIV warns the dishonest plasterer that the Provost will be called in and action will be taken. 'If a plasterer puts anything which he should not into his plaster, he must be fined 5 sous which are to be paid to the master each time he is found out. If the plasterer habitually cheats and if he will not mend his ways, the master can deprive him of his craftsman's status; and if the plasterer will not leave the guild, the master must inform the Provost of Paris, and the Provost must make the plasterer forswear his craft in his presence.'

When, in 1972, the author was invited to hold a seminar in the school of architecture at the University of Southern California (U.S.C.) in Los Angeles, his students agreed most readily to write essays on the theme of the historical parallels suggested to them. These included:

1. The cathedrals and the Los Angeles freeways.

2. Villard de Honnecourt and Frank Lloyd Wright, Le Corbusier, Wachsmann, Gropius, Nervi.

3. Restrictive practices in the building industry in the Middle Ages and in the twentieth century in the United States.

A student who chose the first of these themes concluded his essay by asserting that, like the cathedrals, the freeways would never be finished. One who dealt with restrictive practices drew astounding parallels between Parisian plasterers at the end of the thirteenth century and American plasterers in the 1970s.

The cathedral builders paid taxes and a close look at the tax register held by the municipality of Paris in the thirteenth century reveals some interesting facts. In the year 1292 the names of the 15,200 taxpayers subject to the *taille* were recorded, with their addresses, street by street and parish by parish, as were the sums they paid. The *taille* was a tax levied on people who were neither noblemen nor ecclesiastics and who were not exempt for any other reason. In that year Gandoufle le Lombard paid the highest sum of 114 pounds, 10 sous. The lowest sum of 12 deniers was paid by the 'small people'. The roll is filled with mathematical mistakes which a child under ten would not make nowadays. But there can be no suspicion of fraud as the mistakes are sometimes in favour of the auditor and sometimes not. This lack of precision, which seems to characterize the Middle Ages and which is even found in building, appears shocking to the modern mind which hungers after detail, figures and statistics. This fault is largely compensated for by the feeling for harmony and synthesis which prevailed at the time. The modern man analyses and specializes and the results of thinking exclusively in this fashion are beginning to be felt.

To quote another document: 'The "small people" beyond the Saint-Honoré gate and from the parish of Saint-Germain pay 1 sou each. Guillaume de Laingny, potter, 1 sou. Guillaume, the shoemaker, 1 sou. Jehan Pasquier, the mason, 1 sou. Robert, the roofer, 1 sou. Symon, the glassworker, 1 sou. Raoul, the tapestry-maker, 1 sou,' . . . and so forth. It was only necessary to count how many of the 'small people' were taxed to calculate the total paid by them. The sum quoted in the manuscript is out by 1 pound and 99 sous. The manuscript indicates a total of 14 pounds and 4 sous, whereas Géraud who studied the

Notre-Dame de Paris: a cathedral builder.

This unusual tool was used for rough-hewing stone.

document in the nineteenth century only accounted for 12 pounds, 5 sous.

There are 192 people whose business concerns stonework on the roll of the *taille*. They can be subdivided into 104 masons, 12 stonecutters, 36 plasterers, 8 mortar makers, 2 dressers, 18 quarrymen, 7 mason's assistants, 3 pickmen, 2 pavers.

There is a vast difference in taxes paid by plasterers; they differ from 12 deniers to 4 pounds, 12 sous. 'Raoul paid 1 sou. Symon paid 2 sous. Ysabel, the plasterer, 3 sous. Roger paid 4 sous. Houdée, the plasterer, 5 sous. Colin paid 6 sous. Jehan paid 8 sous. Henri paid 10 sous. Jehan paid 12 sous. Master Yves, the plasterer, 16 sous . . . Raoul paid 3 pounds, 10 sous . . . Dame Marie, the plasterer and 2 children, 4 pounds, 12 sous.'

Raoul and Dame Marie, more likely than not, owned gypsum quarries. There were large deposits of gypsum around Paris, particularly near Montmartre. Parisian plaster was much sought after and it was even exported to England. Indeed, this gypsum is still referred to today as plaster of Paris.

Several women's names crop up among the plasterers and even, although more rarely, among the masons, as these crafts were, relatively speaking, not too arduous. Naturally there were no women among the stonecutters and quarrymen. Dame Marie, the plasterer, who paid 4 pounds, 12 sous for herself and her two children, was not, however, a labourer. She must have inherited the business from her husband. In the thirteenth century women had more legal rights than later French women, who were handicapped by Roman law. Even married women paid taxes on their own incomes in their own names: 'Roger, the stonecutter, 16 sous. His lady, 5 sous.'

The wife was included in contracts signed by her husband and, on his death, she could deal directly with the Church in affairs concerning real estate. In 1225 Raingarde, the widow of Master Arnoul, the stonecutter from Rheims, sold a house to the church of Saint-Symphorien and to Clarambard, a canon of Rheims. She undertook at the same time to have her son Raoulet, then a minor, ratify the sale as soon as he attained his majority. She gave another house – situated in the Rue Saint-Étienne – as security for this.

Preachers and moralists of the Middle Ages slandered women and denied their active role in society. But we should recognize that women, too, contributed to the success of the 'cathedral crusade'.

Mortar makers, like plasterers, paid varying taxes. 'Marguerite, 1 sou; Richard, 2 sous; Robert, 3 sous, Vincent, 5 sous; Guerin, 1 pound; Pierre, 2 pounds.' But it should be pointed out that these people probably did two jobs. Near the Seine, in Paris, there was a street called Rue de la Mortellerie where mortars and perfect, polished vases were made from lias, a blue limestone from the Paris region. It was delicate work, requiring a long apprenticeship, and paragraph XVI of Étienne Boileau's statute was probably addressed to men who did this work. 'Mortar makers may not take on an apprentice for less than six years.'

Paragraph XXI also refers to them: 'Mortar makers are exempt from the watch and all stonecutting since the time of Charles Martel, as men of integrity have heard it passed from father to son.' Exemption from the watch was an important privilege. It cannot logically be supposed that men who simply made mortar needed a six-year apprenticeship or that they would be granted the rarely accorded favour of exemption from the watch. Therefore, mortar makers who actually fashioned stone mortars from lias should be distinguished from simple labourers who made mortar from the same stone.

The quarrymen, makers of stone mortars and stonecutters constituted one branch of the family of stone workers. Plasterers, makers of mortar and masons made up the other branch. Étienne Boileau's statutes confirm this. 'The mortar maker and the plasterer are of the same rank and belong in every way to the same masons' lodge.'

The mason is, above all, a stone setter or layer. English words designating different workmen are interesting in that they reveal the origin of the word 'freemason' and make it clear how the 'operative' freemasonry which preceded the present-day 'speculative' freemasonry came into being and developed. We will return later to this controversial question.

A stained-glass window was given to the cathedral at Bourges by the masons, and another was given by the stonecutters. Masons often appear in medallions, usually working on the walls with their trowel, vertical level and the plumb line, while at the bottom of the walls mortar makers mix mortar and labourers lift the mortar or the stones up to the masons.

In winter masons no longer feature in the accounts, as fear of frost prevented

Bourges: the stained-glass window donated by the masons.

stone-laying. Before leaving the site, the masons took care to cover the tops of the walls with straw or manure to protect the stones and the joints from rain-water. Some of the better stonecutters were employed in the workshop, or lodge, at the foot of the building; others went to work in quarries and, finally, some of the married ones returned to their wives who might be running a smallholding. Sometimes they hired their farm carts to the chapter to carry stones from the quarries to the site.

Although the mason's annual wage was less than that of a stonecutter, who was employed all the year round, his wage by the day was about the same. According to the accounts of the Augustinian convent in Paris, masons and stonecutters earned an average of 22 deniers a day. 'To three stonecutters, five days each, 27 sous, 6 deniers. Or 22 deniers a day . . . To Regnaut de Senlis and Jehan de Meudon, masons, four days each at 22 deniers a day, 15 sous, 4 deniers.' (This is one of the many mathematical errors already mentioned. It should be 14 sous, 8 deniers and not 15 sous, 4 deniers.)

Masons were given certain privileges. The overseer provided them with gloves to protect their hands from burning by lime; they were given a bonus when they completed something or when the keystone was put in position.

Some of the better-off masons, registered for the *taille*, like Gefroi and Symon de Baine who paid 1 pound, 4 sous and 2 pounds, 8 sous respectively, could be employed to supervise small sites.

The 104 masons listed in 1292, numbers of them no doubt working on Notre-Dame de Paris, lived a long way from each other and were spread out all over Paris. Renaud the mason and Jehan Pasquier lived, like the 'small people', 'beyond the Saint-Honoré gate and in the parish of Saint-Germain l'Auxerrois'. Gautier the mason, Simon Lorenz and Tibaut lived in the Rue du Pilori, by the abbey. Pierre the mason lived in the Rue de la Boucherie.

The accounts for Westminster Abbey for the year 1253 (see table overleaf) confirm certain facts which we have already mentioned, notably the irregularity of work for labourers. During the week beginning 14 July, 215 labourers were engaged on the site; the following week 65 were sent away, and in the week beginning 28 July, a further 10 were not employed. With the coming of winter the number of labourers on the site fell spectacularly, to 37 and even to 30 in the week beginning 19 November. The number of masons was also drastically reduced as winter approached. There were 33 in the week beginning 27 October and only 5 two weeks later. It is interesting to note, on the other hand, that the number of smiths hardly varied throughout the year.

This table is also interesting because it gives the number of men working on the site of a large church all the year round. The maximum number of workmen employed was 428 in the week beginning 23 June, and the minimum was 100 during the week beginning 10 November. The average over the whole year is 300. The number is high for a church building.

On a lay site figures could be considerably higher since military interests might play a part. When Beaumaris Castle was built in Wales between 1278 and 1280, 1,630 workmen were employed: 400 masons, 30 smiths and carpenters, 1,000 labourers and 200 carters. The number of specialized workmen on this site was comparatively low – 25% – whereas on a church site, like Westminster Abbey, there would be 50%.

One important contributor to the 'cathedral crusade' was the often forgotten quarryman. He has hardly even been heard of. He was not present on the site and seemed to live outside the community. Very few writers even mention him. In the first place, Étienne Boileau forgot him in his statutes. But the quarryman spent his youth and lost his health down the quarries. His life was hard as he often worked in bad conditions. He suffered from humidity in many quarries and silicosis struck if he worked underground. He was badly paid, barely better than a labourer. On the Paris register the quarrymen, Guillaume, Pierre, Renaut and Jehan, come under the heading of 'small people' who only paid 12 deniers. Medieval men learnt about stone in the quarries, and it was there that they did their apprenticeship. No tradition had survived from antiquity to teach them about the qualities and defects of the material. They had to teach themselves to

MEN EMPLOYED AT WESTMINSTER ABBEY IN 1253

Weeks	Stone-cutters	Monu-mental Masons	Masons	Carpenters	Sanders	Smiths	Glass-makers	Roofers	Labourers	Total
Feb. 1–April 18 (11 weeks)	74	45	24	4	13	20	15		131	326
April 28–May 4	29	14	20	32	13	19	14	4	150	295
May 5–12	39	15	26	32	13	19	14	4	176	338
May 12–18	39	15	26	32	15	17	14	6	200	364
May 19–25	41	16	31	32	15	17	13	6	213	384
May 26–June 1	41	16	31	32	15	17	13	6	213	384
June 2–8	41	16	35	33	15	18	13	6	213	390
June 9–15										
June 16–22	42	18	28	33	15	17	14	4	220	391
June 23–29	53	49	28	28	15	17	14	4	220	428
June 30–July 6	56	49	28	23	15	17	14	4	220	426
July 7–13	60	49	14	21	15	17	13	4	215	408
July 14–20	60	49	14	16	15	17	6	4	215	396
July 21–27	66	49	14	16	15	17	6	4	140	327
July 28–Aug. 3	68	49	14	16	15	16	6	4	130	321
Aug. 4–10	78	49	14	16	15	16	6	4	135	333
Aug. 11–17	68	49	14	16	15	16	2		138	318
Aug. 18–24	68	49	14	16	15	16	2		138	318
Aug. 25–31	49	31	13	13	15	18	2		91	232
Sept. 1–7	49	31	13	13	15	18	2		91	232
Sept. 8–14	49	15	13	13	15	18	2		91	216
Sept. 15–21	56	15	23	13	15	18	2		108	250
Sept. 22–28	58	14	26	13	15	18	3		120	267
Sept. 29–Oct. 5	60	14	31	14	15	18	3		155	310
Oct. 6–12	42	14	31	14	15	18	3		155	292
Oct. 13–19	58	26	33	15	16	18	3	1	158	328
Oct. 20–26	58	15	33	14	15	18	2	1	157	313
Oct. 27–Nov. 2	58	15	33	14	15	18	2		140	295
Nov. 3–9	58	11	11	14	16	18	2		140	270
Nov. 10–16	34	7	5	9		13	2		30	100
Nov. 17–23	35	7	5	9		13	2	2	35	106
Nov. 24–30	35	7	4	9		13	2	2	37	109
Dec. 1–6	35	7	4	9		13	2	2	37	109

recognize the bedding layers and the quality and grain of the stone.

The quarryman was particularly important in the first phase of each new building. He had to excavate millions of cubic metres of stone essential to the foundations. Besides, the quarryman's work often began before the site had even opened. Thus, when in 1277 Edward I founded, at the Crown's expense, the last Cistercian abbey, Vale Royal in Cheshire, Walter of Hereford, who was responsible for the works, sent workmen to the quarries before the site itself was opened.

Quarrymen worked in groups of eight, each group being supervised by a master quarryman. In three years, from 1278 to 1281, precisely 35,448 cartloads of stone were taken from the quarry to the site, over a distance of five miles. If each cartload is estimated to weigh about a ton, then 35,000 tons of stone were excavated by the quarrymen. One cartload must have left the quarry about every quarter of an hour of the working day.

Two English historians, D. Knoop and G.P. Jones, who have analysed in the minutest detail the accounts for these three years, found that although only 5-10% of the masons and stonecutters came from the area, 85% of the quarrymen were local people.

Head quarrymen, like Robert of Inis, Paul of Alueton or Richard Louekin, earned 50% more than the men under them. The figure is given in percentages to avoid confusion between Parisian and English sous and deniers, which were not of equal value. Master quarrymen were usually paid per stone excavated. Reference to the fabric account at Autun shows that Robert Clavel paid Maître Chevillard, master quarryman, so much per stone depending on the size of the stone. So Maître Chevillard received 10 pounds for 1,000 stones, 2 pounds, 9 sous, 6 deniers for 150 stones and 4 pounds for 200 stones. This works out at a little over 2 deniers per stone in the first group, 4 deniers in the second and 5 deniers for stones in the third group.

Some people described as 'quarrymen' in the accounts were really contractors who had bought or hired quarries which they operated. These were men of standing. According to the 1292 register, Asce the quarryman paid 6 pounds in tax, that is 120 times more than the quarrymen Guillaume, Pierre and Jehan. Asce was clearly not a workman but a quarry contractor. This must also have been the case with men like Thibaut des Halles or Hugon who are mentioned in the Saint-Augustin accounts under the heading of quarrymen: 'To Hugon, quarryman of Notre-Dame des Champs, for large foundation stones, 6 pounds.'

The cost of transporting stones in the Middle Ages was so high that there was considerable advantage to be gained from dressing them in the quarry. In fact it has been estimated that it cost as much to transport a cartload of stones from the quarry to a site a little over ten miles away as to buy it in the quarry. The man in charge of the site therefore often sent stonecutters to the quarry to square stones off according to certain measurements. In those days measurements were taken

The Cistercian abbey at Sénanque in a twelfth-century landscape.

in toises (1.949 m.), in feet (0.324 m.) and in inches (0.027 m.).

Attempts were made in the Middle Ages to standardize the size of stones. So in 1264 the municipality of Douai proclaimed that all *carreaux* – rectangular blocks of stone – coming into the town must measure 8 inches by 6 inches by 8 inches. On the Saint-Augustin site, too, all the stones ordered cost the same, so must have been a standard size.

The workmen were paid by the toise after they had been told the depth and thickness: 'For cutting 128 toises and 4 feet of *carreaux*, piecework, 64 sous . . . For cutting 112½ toises of *carreaux*, piecework, 56 sous, 9 deniers.' Here the workman was paid 6 deniers per toise, but stonecutters were sometimes paid by the day or by the week. It is not always known exactly why some workers were paid by the piece and others by the day. But it seems that when an unknown workman came to the site for employment, he was paid by the piece so that his aptitude and willingness to work could be put to the test, after which he might be paid by the day – which he naturally preferred.

From the many marks engraved by pieceworkers on cathedrals, monasteries, fortified castles and city walls throughout France, it seems that piecework was more common in the twelfth than in the thirteenth century, and more widely spread in Alsace, to the south of the Loire and especially in Provence. It was also more usual on small sites like the Saint-Augustin convent than on large sites like

Top: Position marks at Rheims; *Bottom:* a stonecutter's mark at Chartres.

Chartres or Amiens, where it was almost non-existent. Conscripted men were usually paid on piecework. The walls of Aigues-Mortes are literally covered with pieceworkers' marks, and in 1244 workmen were brought from Alès and made to work at Aigues-Mortes on 'penalty of their person or their goods'. It is thought, too, that the powerful feudal lord of Coucy conscripted workmen to build the fortified castle which was put up very quickly in the thirteenth century. Some sixty different pieceworkers' marks have been found on the walls.

What then were these marks? Every stonecutter had a distinguishing sign which he had to engrave on every stone he cut so that the quality of his work could be checked at the end of the week and so that the number of stones he had squared off could be counted before he was paid. The variety of these marks was considerable. They might be geometric figures like triangles or pentagons, or tools like a pick or a hammer; they could be crosses or the workman's own initial. Some workmen engraved the first three letters of their names, or more exceptionally their whole name. These marks were very roughly engraved in the eleventh and twelfth centuries, but became more refined in the thirteenth century.

Fathers handed their own marks down to their sons, but in the father's lifetime the son would add a mark of his own, like a dash. Gradually these signs acquired a sentimental value, and some of them which can be found on, for instance, the pillars in the nave of Notre-Dame de Paris, or on the pillars in the south transept at Chartres, were put there out of personal pride by stonecutters employed by the day or the week. The pieceworkers' marks came to be like signatures. At the end of the fifteenth century the architect Alexandre de Berneval used to put a five-pointed star after his name. A systematic study of the signs in any one region makes is possible, in exceptional cases, to follow workmen from one site to another.

The large numbers of marks found in monasteries enable us to gauge the number of outside workers brought in to build abbeys. They are to be found at Sylvacane, on the pillars in the nave at Sénanque, at Montmajour, at Fontenay in the Côte-d'Or and on the outside wall of the famous Benedictine church at Issoire. Many of them are on the inner side of the stone and can only be seen when the wall is pulled down. Inside the churches the marks engraved on the facing of the stone could not be seen in the Middle Ages because the walls were covered with frescoes. The mason who built the wall did not have to pay any attention to the marks and they can sometimes be seen upside down on the facing.

Some marks were engraved by the quarrymen, since it was necessary to be able to tell the provenance of the stones if two quarries were supplying one site. It was, in fact, important for the regularity and the future stability of the church to build a wall with stones from one place. The quarrymen's marks also made it possible to repair walls with the appropriate stone. The Romans seem to have

A stonecutter's axe.

Above and below:
Stonecutters' marks.

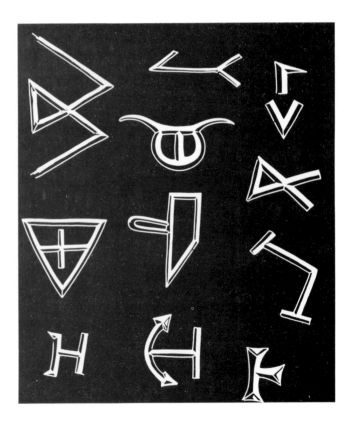

used the same method, for quarrymen's marks can still be seen on Roman buildings.

The quarrymen's and the pieceworkers' marks should not be confused with position marks. When something rather complicated had to be built, the overseer gave the stonecutters specific instructions on how to cut the required blocks. Thus the masons, when the time came, could position the stones correctly before embedding them. The Romans had already used this method, and position marks can be found on the Pont du Gard, for instance. Inscriptions indicate the right position for the blocks: *fronte dextra, fronte sinistra*. So under the fourth arch in the second row can be read: FR.S.II,FR.S.III.FR.S.IIII,FR.D.V. Furthermore, position marks are still used nowadays in modern stone buildings.

Medieval position marks could usually not be seen unless the stones were taken down again. Then it becomes apparent, in the arches for instance, that the stones were marked on one side so that they could be laid as they were cut. When several arches were similarly shaped, each one had a particular mark to distinguish it from the next one. One of the pillars in the smithy at Fontenay has visible position marks.

Position marks were also used to prevent statues from being put in the wrong place. Statues symbolizing the months of the year had been put in the wrong order in Notre-Dame de Paris. The overseer at Rheims was anxious not to make the same mistakes with his 3,000 statues, and he worked out a system of engraved marks so that the mason knew exactly where to place each statue. These marks indicated the side of the cathedral, the doorway where the statue had to go and its exact position in that doorway.

Freemasons and Sculptors

When Walter of Hereford sent his Vale Royal workmen to the quarry, he employed carpenters to build a lodge for the stonecutters with 1,400 planks. The following year he build a second, smaller lodge from 1,000 planks. Whether they were pieceworkers or paid by the week, the stonecutters' lives went on in and around such lodges. In the morning they went there to fetch their tools, they ate their lunch there and in hot weather even had a siesta there. They did not, however, sleep in the lodge. In the cathedral towns workmen could stay either at the inn or in the private houses, while on monastic sites in isolated positions, like Vale Royal, timber houses were built for use as dormitories.

There might be one lodge on a site, or several; one can often see them depicted in contemporary illuminated manuscripts at the foot of buildings under construction. Another important aspect of their usefulness was that during bad weather the stonecutters could work there, particularly in winter when, sheltered from the elements, they could be preparing the work for the masons who would be returning to the site with the fine weather. Gradually the lodges developed into places like clubs, where men not only worked, but discussed problems concerning their craft. They were the origins of masonic lodges and discussions there could become quite animated.

A document in the archives at Notre-Dame de Paris records an incident which occurred in the works lodge on the eve of the Feast of the Assumption. It must have been quite a serious incident as the 1283 statutes mention it with reference to a disagreement over jurisdiction between the bishop and the chapter. The chapter had had to call in armed men to settle the incident. Little by little, the chapters had to regulate the life in the lodges. The oldest known rule was laid down in 1352 by the chapter in York.

The stonecutters and masons were part of a basically itinerant population of workmen. There were many reasons for them to move from site to site and from country to country. The younger men wanted to seek new horizons, to learn a new way of life and different techniques. Amazed by the age in which they lived, they wanted to see the incredible buildings which were springing up all over Christendom. In the space of a year they could hope to find work in turn at, say, Mont-Saint-Michel, Le Mans, Notre-Dame de Paris, Rheims and Strasbourg.

The Portail Royal of Chartres (twelfth century).

In those days there were neither frontiers nor passports and men crossed the Rhine in the east to work in Cologne, or the Channel in the north to work in Canterbury. What a pride and joy it was for the workmen returning home to be able to describe the wonders they had seen. And the villagers remembered them, barely grown up, leaving the family home to work in the neighbouring quarry. Some, urged by their faith, had gone on crusades to the Middle East, where they had built the famous castle of Krak des Chevaliers and other Crusader strongholds to defend the Holy Land. Others wanted to follow celebrated architects who were working in distant places – like the stonecutters who accompanied Étienne de Bonneuil when he set off to build the cathedral at Uppsala.Clearly bachelors were more tempted by these journeys than married men, who stayed closer to their homes so as to be able to return to them at regular intervals.

The life of these builders contrasted with the lives of other medieval workmen who mostly stayed in the same workshops from one year's end to the next and rarely travelled, and then never for professional reasons. Builders who led a wandering life obviously did not do so merely for the pleasure of seeing the country. Some left a site in the hopes of being better paid elsewhere. And often,

Twelfth-century capital at Conques.

for reasons beyond their control, they had to take to the road in search of new work. Perhaps their site had closed, or the overseer, displeased with their work, had dismissed them without warning and without compensation, or perhaps the fabric had run out of money and work was temporarily interrupted. Conscription, too, had the effect of putting men on the road against their wishes, particularly in England, where the King had the power to order sheriffs to recruit twenty-five or forty men for the site of a fortified castle which might be several hundred miles away. Conscription in France did not cause such migrations because no feudal lord, not even the King of France himself, had the authority to recruit men from so far afield.

In the interests of the public and for the sake of a town's commercial reputation, municipalities grew concerned about the settled workers and, from the thirteenth century, in agreement with the heads of various industries, they managed to lay down statutes organizing the professions and forming what later came to be called corporations. Until the municipalities intervened, workers, with a few exceptions, were only grouped into charitable organizations known as brotherhoods, which might be described today as mutual aid societies.

In England, where many statutes like those of York and Coventry have been preserved, there is a marked absence of statutes concerning stonecutters and masons. This can be explained by their itinerant way of life, which meant that these people avoided municipal control. Besides, they worked for the Church and for noblemen who had no desire for them to be professionally organized. It would have been against the interests of the Church for workmen to be able to discuss their conditions of employment and their pay, and against those of the noblemen, since organized groups would perhaps oppose the very convenient system of conscription.

The first English town to make an exception was London, where there is evidence of professional organization of stonecutters and masons in the second half of the fourteenth century. But London was five to ten times larger than York or Coventry, and already had a population of 50,000. There were, predictably, many more builders in London than in a smaller town and they were therefore better prepared to group together and defend their rights. The very size of London made it possible for the municipality to employ these builders regularly, which made them less dependent on their two usual patrons, the Church and feudal lords. It is for this reason that Étienne Boileau's book in Paris has a statute concerning 'masons, stonecutters, plasterers and mortar makers'. Paris was a town with 200,000 inhabitants, whereas Chartres and Amiens had between five and ten thousand. But this forty-eighth statute was peculiar in that it bore the royal stamp. As we noted, the King designated his own master mason, Guillaume de Saint-Patu, as guild master in Paris. Thus the recruiting of men for the royal works was facilitated.

Latin expressions used in the Middle Ages to describe men who cut stone usually make it impossible to distinguish between those who simply cut the

A masterpiece of medieval sculpture: *The Temptation of Eve* from the doorway at Autun. (Musée Rolin.)

stone into blocks and those who carved ribbed vaulting, rose windows or statues for the porches. Sculptors were submerged in the crowd of stonecutters. This obviously seems extraordinary today, for we see a vast difference between the apparently mechanical job of cutting blocks and the heartfelt sculpting of the magnificent statues around the cathedral. The idea that there was an insuperable barrier between the worker and the artist (in the modern sense of the word) only appeared with the Renaissance and was expressed at that time by intellectuals who judged, classified and stratified manual work of which they had no experience.

For the first time in history, Renaissance writers extolled the personal qualities of authors and painters and this resulted in an excessive deification, the consequences of which can still be felt today. The Renaissance invented the idea of the artist. The medieval intellectual, for his part, practically never wrote about specifically aesthetic matters. If he discussed what we choose to call 'art' it was from a theological or philosophical point of view. Certainly, to our knowledge, medieval writers mentioned neither the sculptures which we admire so much, nor their makers – though these were not quite as anonymous as some people would have us believe.

With regard to terminology, it must be pointed out that the avoidance here of the word 'artist' is entirely deliberate. It adds nothing to the glory of the cathedral builders and its present-day meaning was fundamentally alien to the spirit of the Middle Ages. Besides, it was not until 1762 that the *Dictionnaire de l'Académie Française* mentioned the word 'artiste' with the meaning which we understand today.

In England, however, words used to describe stonecutters make it possible to distinguish between those who cut the blocks and those whose work was of a more delicate nature. This distinction is based on the quality of stone used. Those, for instance, who worked with particularly hard stone, like the stone in Kent, were called 'hard hewers' and were distinguished from 'freestone masons', who carved an excellent chalky stone which lent itself to delicate sculpture, and which is found in a wide strip of the country, stretching from Dorset to Yorkshire. Freestone masons were also to be distinguished from 'rough masons'.

The expression 'freestone mason' was gradually replaced by the simpler term 'freemason'. The word 'freemason', then, clearly refers to the quality of the stone and not to some franchise granted to the cathedral builders. When freemasonry was brought from England to France in about 1725, the word 'freemason' was naturally translated as *franc-maçon*, an expression quite unknown to medieval France. On the other hand, there was in London, in 1351, a *maître maçon de franche peer* which is roughly the Anglo-French equivalent of two Latin expressions : *sculptores lapidum liberorum* (London, 1212) and *magister lathomus liberarum petrarum* (Oxford, 1391). The modern English and French translations of this expression would be : 'a master mason of freestone' and '*un maître tailleur de franche pierre*'.

Stained glass at Chartres: sculptors at work.

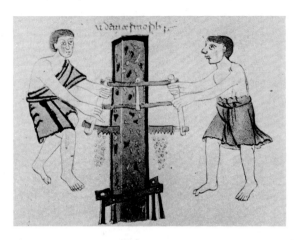
Labourers sawing marble (Raban Maur, *De Origine Rerum*, eleventh century).

The words *'franc'* or *'franche'* ('free') are used in France to this day to describe, stone, and the dictionary, the *Littré*, mentions a *'franc liais'*, which is a beautiful stone for building from the region around Paris. The word is also used to describe stone of excellent quality. In an underground quarry in Paris, an engineer in charge pointed out some very fine stone in the wall of the gallery, describing it to the author as *'bancs francs'*.

In fact sculptures were often made of a different stone from the walls against which they were set. It can be seen at a glance that the famous statues of the Portail Royal at Chartres do not come from the Berchères quarry. At Vézelay the capitals are not built of the same stone as the rest of the church. But then the stonecutters' frequent journeys across the country made it possible for them to assess stone from many different quarries. Some managed to work with the stone which most suited their own talents, and others managed to order a particular stone for certain difficult pieces of work. Given the high costs of transport, we should be thankful for the sympathetic attitudes of those who were prepared to pay.

In any consideration of the sculptor's role in medieval society we naturally want to know what part he played in the choice and execution of masterpieces. On the whole, since old texts tell us nothing, the answer can only be found in a few more or less credible hypotheses; and perhaps one of the best ways of reaching a better understanding of the creators of a given period is to see their craft, whether literary or visual, within its own historical framework. Here we are dealing with techniques of visual expression.

Paleolithic man expressed himself through objects made of bone or through frescoes like the ones at Lascaux, fifth-century Greeks expressed themselves in

Top: A labourer on the left mixes the colour for his master to paint the sculpted group of the Virgin and Child (*Las Cántigas* of Alfonso X, thirteenth century). *Bottom:* Carving a tombstone (Mort du Roi Arthur, *1316*, British Museum).

painting earthenware vases or in sculpture such as the Parthenon frieze, the Byzantines made ivory objects or vast mosaics like those at Santa Sophia, the Renaissance produced bronze statues and easel paintings; and so it continued. These methods of expression make it possible to understand certain facets of the religious and moral thought of the day, and were in a perpetual state of evolution, subjected, as they must have been, to changes of thought and of material conditions. Whereas some methods of expression reach, for a time, heights which we would call great, others lose their privileged position and are reduced to the second-rate or the outdated.

In the tenth and eleventh centuries sculpture was not one of the favoured techniques, in comparison with, say, frescoes, silverwork or miniatures. When, during the eleventh century, thanks to a better knowledge of their craft, stonecutters began to carve small scenes, they were no doubt able to do so without ecclesiastical supervision – little attention can have been paid to their timid and clumsy endeavours. But it seems that their efforts and their improving standards progressively attracted the attention of Christendom to a technique which was new to it; and then monumental sculpture came into being. Born into a society that was steeped in religion, from his earliest childhood the stonecutter heard, both at home and in church, stories which served as themes for his sculpture. There was a certain communal inspiration which explains why almost identical scenes can be found in very different regions.

Monumental sculpture developed rapidly and from the twelfth century became a major means of expression. Around the middle of the century stained glass, in its turn, became very important – at the expense of frescoes, which declined as window areas increased and wall surfaces diminished. In the thirteenth century the fresco became an outdated technique.

Within what limits did the sculptor's freedom develop? It must first of all be pointed out that in an ascendant era creators could not be misunderstood, neither could they disagree with their patrons. There could only be different opinions on points of detail. It is hard to imagine the painters at Lascaux allowing their opinion to prevail over the opinions of the magicians and theologians of the day. The sculptors of the Parthenon could, within limits, discuss the form with the priest, but not the basic essentials. This subjection of creators to magicians or priests went without saying. It was such an obvious principle or tradition that few societies specified it in writing.

A famous text drawn up by the Fathers of the Church at the Council of Nicaea in 787 proves an exception. The extraordinary and passionate quarrel of the Iconoclasts was required for the Church to state what had always been obvious. It was pointed out that 'the composition of religious pictures is not left to the inspiration of the artists, but depends on the principles laid down by the Catholic Church and religious tradition. Art alone is the painter's province, the composition belongs to the Fathers.'

It would be impossible to be more explicit. By having the figure of Christ removed from the choir of the famous church at Assy in Haute-Savoie, the Church was merely applying the principle expressed at the Council of Nicaea twelve centuries earlier. Perhaps this text should be written in capital letters at the entrance to every exhibition of sacred art and circulated among all those whose ambition it is to work for the Church.

By becoming a sculptor, the stonecutter graduated to the intellectual world. He came into contact with theologians and learnt from them; he had the wonderful opportunity of looking through the abbey's precious manuscripts. He learnt to look, to observe and to think. His intellectual horizon broadened, which meant that his carvings benefited both materially and spiritually. Thanks to the miniatures and manuscripts which he had seen and admired in other abbeys, the sculptor could humbly suggest slight variations to themes put forward by the Fathers. As the sculptor and the theologian were working towards the same end, the former could feel free, for within this association there was no compulsion. So it could be said that, unlike the modern artist, the medieval sculptor had no individuality, since he laid no claim to personal inspiration.

However, a justifiable pride overcame these sculptors from humble origins, and they did not hesitate, particularly in the twelfth century, to engrave their names on the stone. Gislebert signed the famous tympanum at Autun 'Gislebertus fecit hoc opus'; Giraud signed the portal of Saint-Ursin at Bourges, Umbert a capital in the porch of Saint-Benoît-sur-Loire and Rettibitus a capital in

The legend of the sculptor Pygmalion: from the *Roman de la Rose*, c. 1370.

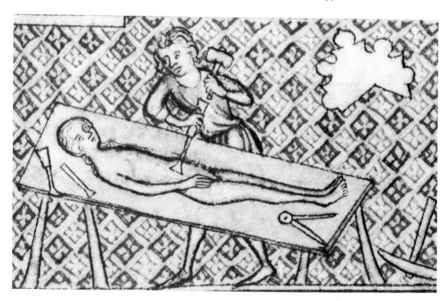

Notre-Dame-du-Port at Clermont. Sculptors were, in fact, not the only ones to sign their work. Durand, the mason, signed one of the keystones in the cathedral at Rouen in about 1233 'Durandus me fecit'. And, in the same cathedral, the glassmaker Clement de Chartres signed his stained glass. The Latin term 'me fecit' must, of course, be treated with care as in some cases it refers not to the workman but to the patron. Nevertheless it is obviously wrong to speak of the anonymity of the cathedral builders. The medieval sculptures are not all signed, but neither are those at Versailles and no one has ever claimed that seventeenth-century sculptors were anonymous.

The sculptor often worked on a stone which had already been embedded in the building; the capitals at Vézelay, for instance, were made this way. The carvings in 1957 on the façade of the church of Saint-Ferdinand-des-Ternes in Paris's 17th Arrondissement were executed in the same way as many twelfth-century works – that is, in position. Thus the sculpture is in perfect harmony with the building. The twelfth-century sculptured columns, like the ones in the Portail Royal at Chartres, demonstrate this close relationship between the sculptor and the architect. Unfortunately, this magnificent harmony did not last long; perhaps the sculptor lost some of his original humility and wanted to work independently and separate his sculpture from the column. He took to carving his piece of stone away from the building, in the lodge. And this is how he can be seen working in the thirteenth-century stained-glass window which he and other stonecutters gave to Notre-Dame de Chartres.

Drunk with his new independence and his amazing intellectual and material success, he wanted to put statues everywhere. He wanted to cover the churches and smother them with statues. Design became confused; some of the 1,200 sculptures in Notre-Dame de Paris were fixed in the wrong position. In Rheims the 3,000 statues had to be numbered like prefabricated products today. Sculptors settled at Tournai and màde statues to order. In 1272 the Abbé de Cambron made a deal with two of them for columns for the windows at Bruges to be made to measure and dispatched.

Having broken with the architect, the sculptor next broke with the theologians. Did he already see himself as a superior being? Was this the beginning of the Renaissance? However it may be, he had to be called to order. The ascendant era of medieval Christianity was coming to an end. In 1306 the sculptor Tideman made a figure of Christ for a London church. The figure was not thought to conform to tradition. The bishop himself intervened actively and had the statue removed from the church. Then he insisted that Tideman pay back the amount he had been paid.

This independence of the sculptor from tradition was unthinkable a century earlier and coincided with the waning of religious faith. The rich and powerful, who in magnificent bursts of generosity had until now given part of their fortunes to cathedrals, began to use their money to improve their personal comfort and satisfy their appetite for pleasure. Large houses and private chapels began to be built. The big building sites were to feel the effects of this. The best sculptors and cathedral builders were tempted away and employed by the great men of the day, to decorate their houses and chapels. It was the kind of thing that must have happened in Athens in the fifth and fourth centuries B.C., when the power of Athens began to decline after the Peloponnesian Wars. Throughout the fifth century sculptors had worked on buildings like the Parthenon; then, in the fourth century, Athens was ruined and rich individuals attracted sculptors like Praxiteles to pander to their egotistic tastes.

But the opportunity for French sculptors to benefit from private patronage was blighted by the outbreak of the Hundred Years' War in 1337. The economy collapsed, the population was decimated by famine, war and the plague. Rich men who could still employ sculptors were few and far between, and in a climate of war sculpture became a luxury. The cathedral sites either closed or worked at half strength; most sculptors were impressed into military service and required to build keeps and fortified castles. The buildings required no delicacy of detail, and stone from local quarries had to be sufficient for them as the transporting of stone over long distances was impracticable because of the dangers on the roads and waterways. Unable to travel around, new generations of workmen forgot the whereabouts of famous quarries which had produced the stone for monumental carving. The grandchildren of the men who built Chartres and Mont-Saint-Michel are hardly recognizable in the unfortunate workmen who were obliged to spend their lives carving out cannon balls.

When the stonecutters began to carve again in the middle of the fifteenth century, despite all their efforts they could not recapture the tradition of the 'cathedral crusade'. The world had moved on and stone carving was out of fashion.

Clermont-Ferrand: a capital from Notre-Dame-du-Port (early twelfth century).

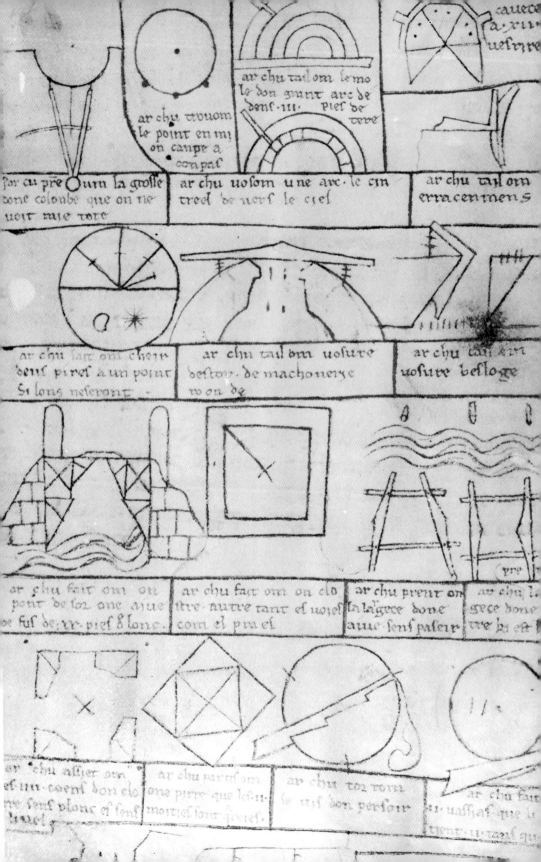

ar chu trouom le point en mi on canpe a conpas

ar chu tail om le mole don grant arc de dens .iii. pies de tere

cauece a .xii. uesnes

par cu prē Oum la grosse done colombe que on ne uoit traie tote

ar chu uosom une arc le cintrel be nerf le ciel

ar chu tail om erracenmens

ar chu fait om cheir dens pires a un point si lons nescront

ar chu tail om uosure destor de machonerie won de

ar chu tail om uosure bestoge

ar chu fait om on point de for one a jue be fus de .xx. pies s long

ar chu fait om on clostre autre tant es uoses com el pra es

ar chu prent om la largece done auec sens paseir

ar chu l gece done tre bi est

ar chu assier om es .iiii. coens bon clo ve sens plone es sens liuel

ar chu parrisom one pirre que lesiiii moities sont ivies

ar chu tor rotu le uis don persoir

ar chu fait ii uassaus que li tient .ii raus qu

The Architects

At the time of the great exhibition of French thirteenth-century illuminated manuscripts in 1955, the Bibliothèque Nationale in Paris exhibited the sketchbook of the thirteenth-century architect Villard de Honnecourt, who came from the small village of Honnecourt, between Cambrai and Vaucelles, in Picardy. This extraordinary document, which contains thirty-three pages of parchment covered on both sides with notes and drawings by the cathedral builder himself, is well known to historians. In the nineteenth century, the architect Lassus edited it and reproduced it in facsimile form with a detailed commentary. This edition can fortunately be found in good libraries, and people interested in the Middle Ages and in architecture can study Villard's sketches without having to refer to the original manuscript in the Bibliothèque Nationale. François Bucher also edited a facsimile edition of Villard's notes, published in the United States in 1979.

It is surprising that most commentators have never so much as bothered to visit Villard's native village. There they would have learnt that at Honnecourt-sur-Escaut a large abbey under the rule of St Columban was founded by some Irish monks in about 670. The abbey was razed to the ground in the tenth century by the Hungarians. At the end of the eleventh century the Pope sent some Benedictines there, and they opened a stone yard for the reconstruction of the monastery. It was probably on this site that Villard became an apprentice builder. The remains of the abbey were destroyed during the First World War. Honnecourt found itself on the front line and only one house escaped destruction. The present village was entirely rebuilt in the 1920s.

It is even more surprising that the inhabitants themselves know nothing of the most famous of their sons. The much-esteemed *Guide Bleu* does not even mention him, nor does any other guide book. In August 1978 there was no mention of Villard at the entrance to the village. In the village, neither road nor square commemorated him. Inside the church, which has been rebuilt but where vestiges of the old abbey can be found, there was a simple notice about the abbey. When asked if she had heard of Villard de Honnecourt, a woman outside the church replied, 'I have heard the name, but I don't know why. You should

Planche 38 of Villard de Honnecourt's *Sketchbook:* geometric diagrams to be used on sites by stonecutters and architects.

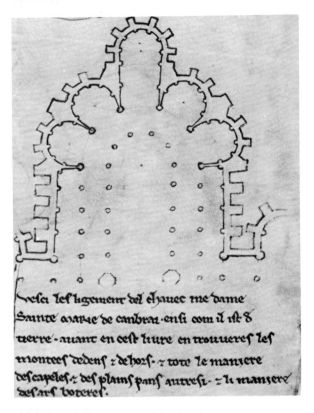

Plan for Cambrai by Villard de Honnecourt.

ask Monsieur le Curé, who lives opposite the church.' Monsieur le Curé had never heard of Villard de Honnecourt, but, he explained, he had only been in the village for two or three years. He suggested asking the mayor. But the mayor pointed out that he was a native of the Paris region and had not heard of the architect. However, he promised that at the next meeting of the municipal council the naming of a square after Villard would be discussed. So the architect had to wait for more than seven centuries for his own village to honour him as he deserved.

Villard's sketchbook is encyclopedic and a real treasury of information. Several plates are fairly well known but of the text, more often than not, Villard's essays on triangulation are all that have been reproduced. From our point of view, the most interesting aspect of the sketchbook is the extent to which it reveals the wide curiosity of a thirteenth-century architect. The feeling for harmony and synthesis which characterized the Middle Ages, in contrast to our own passion for specialization, has already been commented on. To a certain extent, and probably influenced by Le Corbusier, young architects since the war have learnt to understand architecture as a whole. The modern town-planner is

God as the Architect of the Universe: miniature from an Old Testament, French mid-thirteenth century (Vienna).

more like Villard. He studies the problems of his time in breadth. For too long, architects were theorists, only interested in the aesthetics of buildings. The human aspect of modern town-planning can be compared to the human side of an architect like Villard. For all that, the thirteenth-century architect had one advantage over his twentieth-century counterpart: he was more or less brought up on the site and knew how to oversee a building site without needing a contractor.

In his sketchbook Villard introduces himself as follows: 'Villard de Honnecourt greets you and begs all those who are involved in all the different types of work mentioned in this book to pray for his soul and remember him; because this book may be a great help in instructing the principles of masonry and carpentry. You will also find it contains methods of portraiture and line drawing as dictated by the laws of geometry.'

Villard's interest in carpentry deserves comment; though it is unfortunate that the part of his sketchbook that is missing is precisely the item on carpentry. This is a great pity as it would have enabled us to learn more about medieval timber techniques, on which we have relatively few documents. An architect, in those days, had to have a very thorough knowledge of carpentry. The master carpenter was as important as the master mason. Thus, under Philip the Fair, the master carpenter and the master mason earned the same wage and had the same privileges. Whether or not they were present at the palace, they earned four sous a day and a bonus of a hundred sous, payable on All Saints' Day. In addition, they could eat at the palace and had a pair of shod horses and the palace smithy at their disposal.

As Lassus says, the subjects dealt with in the sketchbook can be classified as follows: 1. Mechanics; 2. Practical geometry and trigonometry; 3. Carpentry; 4. Architectural design; 5. Ornamental design; 6. Diagrams; 7. Furniture design; 8. Subjects which are alien to the specialized knowledge of the architect and draughtsman.

Originally the manuscript was really Villard's notebook in which he jotted down for future reference things which interested him. Hahnloser noticed that the handwriting is not always the same and he concluded that the notebook, which was initially personal, must have become a lodge sketchbook. After Villard's death it must have passed into the hands of other architects who added drawings and some remarks.

Villard de Honnecourt worked in the region where he was born. He has left us a drawing of the chevet of the church at Vaucelles near Honnecourt, which he is said to have rebuilt. 'Here is the plan,' he wrote of the chevet of Madame Sainte Marie de Cambrai, 'just as it rises from the ground. Later in this book you will find plans of the elevations, including the positioning of all the side chapels, the walls and the designs for the flying buttresses.'

This cathedral was destroyed at the beginning of the nineteenth century, but

Masons playing dice.

by an extraordinary piece of luck, and thanks to a photograph of a no longer existing model of Cambrai, we can admire the choir which was built at the time of Villard, perhaps by the master himself. This model was one of a secret collection of models of strategically important towns and their immediate surroundings. The models, which were Louis XIV's idea, were obviously kept from the public and from foreign diplomats. They continued to be made throughout the eighteenth century and even in part of the nineteenth century. Today they have no military importance and make a very worthwhile display in the Musée des Plans-Reliefs which is temporarily housed on the top floor of the Hôtel des Invalides. When Paris was occupied in 1815, the Germans took the opportunity to remove some of these models, including the one of Cambrai and its cathedral, to Berlin, where it was put in the Zeughaus. Unfortunately it was destroyed during the bombing of Berlin in 1944. The photograph of the model is all that remains of the cathedral.

Like other stonecutters and architects of his day, Villard travelled a good deal and, thanks to his sketchbook, we can follow some of his journeys. He visited Rheims, where he sketched the elevations of the cathedral. In Chartres he drew the rose window on the west front and the labyrinth (which he copied back to front). He went to Meaux and Laon, where he quite rightly admired the famous cathedral towers. He took care to draw the oxen which are still positioned so strangely at the corners of these towers. He went to Switzerland, where he visited Lausanne and drew one of the rose windows in the cathedral. He then crossed Germany on his way to Hungary. He says himself, 'Here is one of the windows which is between two pillars in the nave at Rheims; I had been summoned to Hungary when I drew it because I liked it.' In Hungary he was asked to build the cathedral church dedicated to St Elizabeth at Kosice (now in Czechoslovakia).

During his travels Villard sketched at random hundreds of things which interested him. He was a close observer of nature and drew animals and insects like cicadas, dragonflies, bees and snails; he drew birds and hares and hedgehogs, cats, dogs and horses. He even drew caged animals, a lion cub, lions and bears, and fantastic animals like the dragon. These drawings served as models, either for himself, or for the sculptors who worked for him. And for the same reason he drew numerous people, taking particular care over the folds of their clothes. He drew a Crucifixion with the figures of St John and the Virgin Mary, a Descent from the Cross, which in those days was an unusual scene, a Virgin and Child, and the Twelve Apostles. And also, beside these holy figures, he drew two dice players, probably masons playing on a mortar-board, and two wrestlers. He also drew nudes.

Some of these drawings were clearly inspired by antiquity and he even reproduced some fragments from Ancient Rome. There were more Roman remains then than now, and there was a fairly close link between the Middle Ages and antiquity. With very few exceptions, all the Latin works were known to well-read men. But there was then none of the, at times, uncritical and often systematic admiration of the Renaissance for anything remotely concerned with antiquity.

It has been noted that some of Villard's most frequently reproduced drawings concern triangulation. Too much attention should not be paid to this hasty method of drawing. It is merely for convenience.

Villard was interested in minor inventions – what some would call 'gadgets'; indeed the Middle Ages as a whole seem to have liked them. Villard wanted gadgets everywhere, even in church : 'In this way,' he wrote, 'the eagle's head can be made to turn towards the deacon when the gospel is read.' He also drew and described a hand-warmer which he intended for the bishop. 'This device is good for a bishop, he can boldly attend High Mass; if he holds it in his hands he will be warm so long as the fire lasts. It is made in such a fashion that whichever way up it is, the little stove inside is always straight.' The same system was used later to keep naval compasses horizontal and barometers vertical.

Villard explains in detail the workings of a hydraulic toy which was highly fashionable at the time, a contraption made on the principles of a siphon. On another page he tells us that, thanks to a carefully explained clockwork movement, 'an angel can be made to keep its finger perpetually pointed at the sun.'

Villard de Honnecourt: water-powered saw, the first automatic double-acting machine; crossbow; diagram for clock movement; lifting device with screw and lever; mobile eagle for lectern.

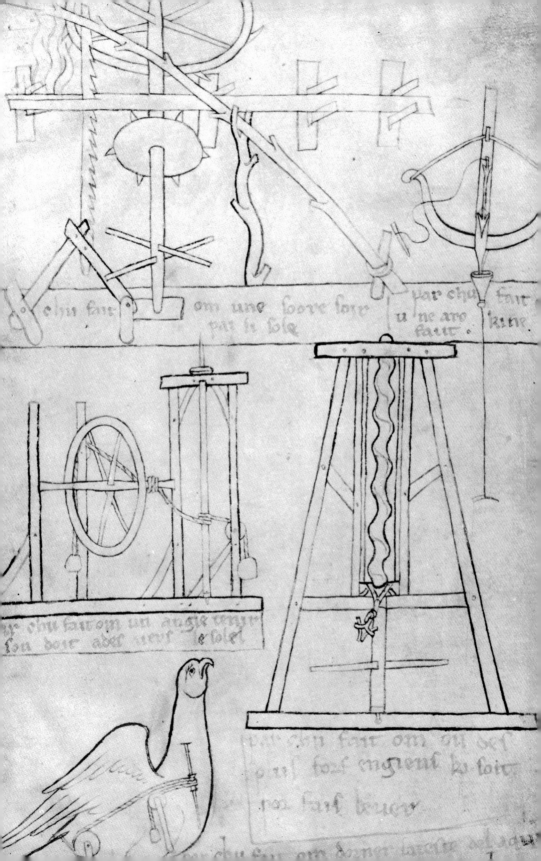

chu fait · om une soore soir par li sole · par chu fait une aro fait · kine

par chu faitoni un angle tenir son doit abet lieux le solei

par chu fait om ou del puis fort engient la soir · por fait tenir

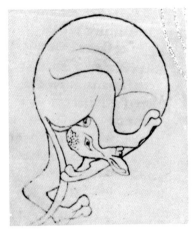

Sketches from nature.

But Villard was not only interested in these gadgets. As an engineer he was passionately involved in far more important problems – for instance, in machines for lifting weights. He invented one with a screw and a lever : 'In this way,' he wrote, 'the most powerful machine for lifting weights can be made.' He also made it possible for overseers to prepare their work: 'In this way an oblique arch should be cut . . .' 'In this way the springers in the vault should be cut . . .' 'In this way keystones should be cut : place them upside down . . .

Medieval miniatures show winches and capstans worked by men which must have been similar to those used by the Romans. It is known that the inclined plane system used by the Egyptians to put up the Pyramids was practically never used in cathedral buildings. The houses which surrounded the churches made the method impossible.

Large treadwheels inside which one or two men walked like squirrels were commonly used to raise materials to the tops of buildings. The muscular effort needed to make these wheels turn and the system work was not excessive. Some of these large wheels can still be seen, at Mont-Saint-Michel, in the vaults of the cathedral at Beauvais and in some churches in Alsace. They were occasionally left in position when the sites were closed so that materials for repairs could be brought up later. The master carpenters were in charge of inventing and making the hoisting machines. As these were expensive to assemble they were not dismantled when work was finished and the chapters could then hire them out.

Villard applied himself to difficult problems like the cutting of wood under water. In his sketchbook he drew a device which he invented for the purpose : 'In this way piles can be cut back under water and platforms laid on them.' He took care to point out on his drawing that a level and a plumb line would have to be used to ensure that the mechanism was vertical.

Like many others after him, he attempted to make perpetual motion machines which would free men from the servitude of manual labour : 'Many are the days when masters have argued over how to make a wheel turn by itself; this is how it can be done with uneven hammers or quicksilver.' He was clearly mistaken

Hoisting devices: large treadwheel and pulley (*Histoire Universelle*, second half of thirteenth century).

about the perpetual motion machines, but at least he conceived of a semi-automatic machine which effectively replaced man's muscular strength in cutting wood: 'In this way a saw can be made to saw on its own.' Hydraulic power, which the Middle Ages made so much use of, drove the mechanism.

Villard's interest in geometry is continually evident. 'Here begins the drawing method for the diagram as it is dictated by the art of geometry, to facilitate the work . . .' 'These four pages contain geometrical designs, but for them to be understood they must be studied with care . . .' 'All these diagrams are geometrical layouts . . .' 'It is thanks to geometry that the height of a building or the width of a river can be measured . . .' 'In this way the height of the tower can be measured . . .' 'In this way the width of a piece of water can be measured, without its having to be crossed . . .' 'In this way two jars can be made, one of which contains twice the quantity of the other.'

Lassus studied Villard's grasp of geometry and he noticed that, for instance, 'the determination of the centre of a circle from three fixed points on the circumference and the proving of a right angle with a set square indicate a knowledge of the properties of a circle and of perpendiculars. The measurement of the distance between two points or of the height of a tower is based on the equality of triangles in certain given conditions; the problem of a vase with twice the capacity of another is based on the measurement of a circle and the theorem of the square on the hypotenuse. Plans for a cloister presuppose a knowledge of the properties of the diagonals of a rectangle.'

A close study of the correspondence of 1025 between two ecclesiastical scholars, Ragimbold de Cologne and Radolf de Liège, is very enlightening about geometric knowledge in the eleventh century, and proves that almost all Greek documents had been lost during the early Middle Ages. It turns out that the correspondents themselves were unable to work out any geometric theorem. The historian Paul Tannery has concluded that 'analysis of these letters reveals admissions of ignorance'. Ragimbold and Radolf discussed the definition of an outside angle of a triangle (a word which they found in one of the few old works in their possession) without coming to any agreement. Neither of them could manage to demonstrate correctly the theorem proving that two right angles equal the sum of the angles of a triangle. A few years later Francon de Liège was still looking for a solution to the same problem, and he revealed that other scholars, Wazron, Razegan and Adelman, had applied themselves to it. So several generations attempted in vain to solve the same relatively simple problem.

Since this shows that medieval scholars did not re-invent geometry and that Greek documents had almost entirely disappeared from Western Europe, where then did men like Villard de Honnecourt discover their science?

Some of it must have been handed down to them directly from Roman geometers or they must have learnt it from studying the works of Vitruvius, the

Villard de Honnecourt: top left, a mechanism for sawing wood under water.

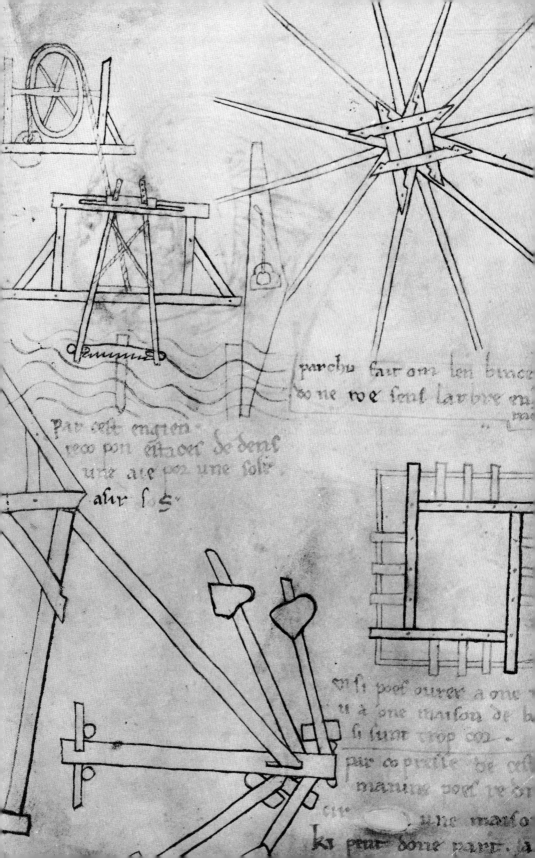

parchu fair om len buuer
so ne roe sent larbre en
vaie

par cest engien
veo pon estaoie de deue
une ate per une soit
asir f. s.

vl si poet ourer a one
u a one maison de b
si sunt trop coo .
par co piaste be ces
manire poet re on
cir . une maiso
ki puit sone part. a

Roman architect from the time of Augustus whose manuscripts were frequently recopied during the early Middle Ages. But we believe that most architects gained their knowledge from Arab science. In fact, during the ninth and tenth centuries, Muslim scholars had translated into Arabic a considerable number of scientific works from classical antiquity, namely the writings of Aristotle, Plato, Euclid and Ptolemy. The Arabs produced a magnificent synthesis of the knowledge of classical antiquity and of India; they assimilated the arithmetic, developed chemistry and algebra and more or less invented trigonometry. This vast culture was taught indiscriminately to Muslims, Christians and Jews in Arab universities in Spain throughout the eleventh and twelfth centuries. Raymond, the Archbishop of Toledo from 1126 to 1151, founded a school of translators to translate Greek and Arab texts into Latin. Thus Adelard of Bath translated the complete works of Euclid at a time when only a few theorems were known in Europe. In 1145 Robert of Chester translated Al-Khawarizmi's work on algebra. This date marks the introduction of algebra into Europe. Gerard of Cremona translated Ptolemy's *Almagest* and Al-Zarqali's works on trigonometry which prove the importance of sines and tangents. Plato's *Meno* and *Phaedo* were also translated.

So, by the middle of the twelfth century, Greek and Arab science was available to Western European scholars. The remarkable Arab contribution to our culture is often underestimated, and yet it was this that made the full flowering of the Middle Ages possible. Without it the Renaissance could barely have developed and the twentieth century might still be technically and scientifically in the nineteenth century.

Presumably men like Villard de Honnecourt or his twelfth-century predecessors could learn this science in schools in Paris or Chartres, and they could also study manuscripts in Latin or in the Picardy dialect. Thierry de Chartres and Guillaume de Conches both taught in the school at Chartres in the middle of the twelfth century, and both were familiar with Aristotle's theories of physics. On the other hand some Latin scientific works were translated into Romance or into the Picardy dialect, perhaps for the use of technicians like the cathedral builders. One of these thirteenth-century manuscripts written in Villard de Honnecourt's own dialect has survived, and it can be consulted in the Bibliothèque Sainte-Geneviève in Paris. The author is concerned with mathematical problems:
'To find the area of an equilateral triangle . . .' 'To find the area of an octagon . . .' 'To find the number of houses in a round city . . .' The solutions to these problems are commented on in detail and accompanied by explanatory diagrams. The style and spirit of these texts is to be found in Villard de Honnecourt's writings : 'In this way the central point of a circle drawn with a compass can be found. . .' 'In this way the thickness of a column, only part of which is visible, can be calculated. . .' 'And for a good wooden vault, pay attention to the following.'

It cannot be claimed that Villard, or other architects of his time, had a very thorough comprehension of geometry, trigonometry or algebra; learning for these builders must have been above all empirical. But it would seem that contact with this science must have contributed to the mathematical precision required in drawing the plans and elevations of these great cathedrals.

Two drawings of assembled squares from *planche* 38 of the sketchbook deserve special attention. Under the one in the centre of the plate is written : ' In this way a cloister with its gallery and courtyard can be drawn.' This drawing is not explicit and needs a commentary. The area of the outer square is twice as big as that of the inner square and this has been achieved by means of tracing the diagonal of the small square and by building another square on to this diagonal. It will be noticed that this second square is double the size of the first : the first square has, then, been doubled. Next, the new square has been placed outside the first one. The area of the cloister garden is therefore half the size of the whole cloister, the proportion being 1 to 2, an elementary proportion which is often found in medieval buildings. The builders preferred simple ratios (double and half; treble and a third). Since measurements varied from town to town, architects did not put a scale on their plans and they were particularly interested in proportions which could easily be translated without recourse to a conversion table.

Under the square almost immediately below the cloister plan is written the following explanation : 'In this way a stone can be divided so that both halves are square.' This cannot be taken literally since stones have never been halved in this way. Diagonal lines joining the middle of the sides have been drawn across a square. Thus the inside square is half the size of the outer square.

The interesting thing about these drawings is not immediately evident and nothing about them seems especially striking. Indeed, for Villard and 'Magister 2' (who is supposed to have taken over the sketchbook, presumably on Villard's death), these drawings appear no more important than some twenty other diagrams on the same page. But interest in them may be stimulated by a work of a German architect, Wenzel Roriczer, an extraordinary document which was printed with the bishop's approval two centuries later, in 1486, in Regensburg. The work is entitled *On the Correct Building of Pinnacles*. The likeness of Roriczer's diagrams to those on *planche* 38 of Villard's sketchbook is immediately striking. Roriczer's drawings are more detailed and more explicit, although rather difficult to understand for anyone whose knowledge of geometry is limited or who is unfamiliar with the problems of building. Roriczer explains how to draw a pinnacle correctly. Using Villard's method, he makes a square inside another square. Inside the second square he puts a third square; the squares are superimposed one on the other, as in Villard's diagram, and little by little a pinnacle takes shape.

The reason for taking such a close interest in this is that Roriczer claimed to be revealing the secrets of masonry. So, according to this architect, the secrets of masonry lie in the art of taking an elevation from a diagram. The method of making pinnacles was in reality generally used in the building of cathedrals. Why was so much importance attached to it?

A document dated 1459 confirms Roriczer's assertion. In that year master stonecutters from such cities as Strasbourg, Vienna and Salzburg met at Regensburg to standardize the statutes of their lodges. Among other things, they declared that no one should reveal to the outside world the art of taking an elevation from a plan : 'No workman, no master, no journeyman will tell anyone who is not of the craft and who has never been a mason how to take an elevation from a plan.'

Both Roriczer's document and the 1459 one have often misled historians who have reached hasty conclusions concerning the masons' secret or secrets. What was a secret in the fifteenth century was not necessarily one in the thirteenth century. Professional organizations changed profoundly between the twelfth and thirteenth centuries. The reader's attention has been drawn to the break which the end of the thirteenth century represents in medieval history and the history of building. From this date architects organized themselves profession-ally and gradually came to agreements not to disclose technical and scientific knowledge which they had learnt through outside contacts during the ascendant period of the Middle Ages.

Planche 38 proves that Villard de Honnecourt knew the principle of taking an elevation from a plan, but, as a thirteenth-century architect, he did not regard it as a secret. Besides, university professors who taught geometry – which was one of the seven liberal arts – taught the students Plato's method of duplicating a square. This can be found in the *Meno* in a dialogue between Socrates and a slave. This passage from Plato was indirectly the basis of the method used for

Details from *planche 38*.

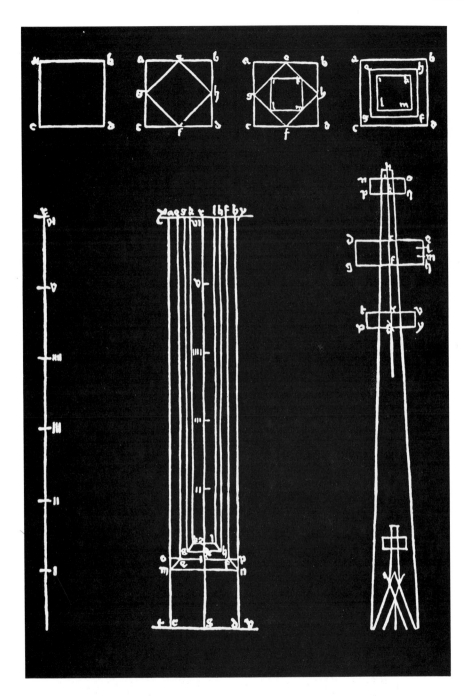

Plan and elevation of a pinnacle according to Roriczer.

taking an elevation from a plan and of the fifteenth-century stonecutters' secret. Nearly 2,000 years separate Plato from Roriczer. Under the circumstances it may be interesting and indeed moving to hear Socrates addressing the slave-boy:*

SOCRATES. Now, boy, you know that a square is a figure like this?
(*Socrates begins to draw figures in the sand at his feet. He points to the square* ABCD.)

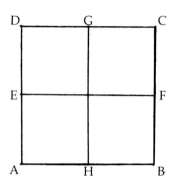

BOY. Yes
SOCRATES. It has all these four sides equal?
BOY. Yes.
SOCRATES. And these lines which go through the middle of it are also equal? [The lines EF,GH.]
BOY. Yes.
SOCRATES. Such a figure could be either larger or smaller, could it not?
BOY. Yes.
SOCRATES. If this side is two feet long, and this side the same, how many feet will the whole be? Put it this way. If it were two feet in this direction and only one in that, must not the area be two feet taken once?
BOY. Yes.
SOCRATES. But since it is two feet this way also, does it not become twice two feet?
BOY. Yes.
SOCRATES. And how many feet is twice two? Work it out and tell me.
BOY. Four.
SOCRATES. Now could one draw another figure double the size of this, but similar, that is, with all its sides equal like this one?
BOY. Yes.
SOCRATES. How many feet will its area be?
BOY. Eight.

*In the translation by W. K. C. Guthrie.

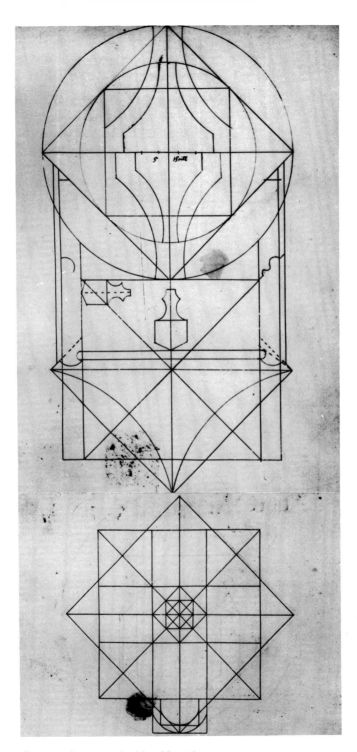

Drawings by Lorenz Lechler, fifteenth-century master mason.

Drawings by Villard de Honnecourt, to be compared with (*opposite*) Giotto's *Joachim's Dream* in the Scrovegni Chapel, Padua.

This dialogue of Plato's did not escape the notice of the Romans and of Vitruvius, who speaks about it. So the cathedral builders could have learnt about the duplication of the square in the university, but also, quite simply, by reading Vitruvius's *De Architectura*. Here is what Augustus's architect wrote* and this was certainly known by the medieval stonecutters:

First of all, among the many very useful theorems of Plato, I will cite one as demonstrated by him. Suppose there is a place or a field in the form of a square and we are required to double it. This has to be effected by means of lines correctly drawn, for it will take a kind of calculation not to be made by means of mere multiplication. The following is the demonstration. A square place ten feet long and ten feet wide gives an area of one hundred feet. Now if it is required to double the square, and to make one of two hundred feet, we must ask how long will be the side of that square so as to get from this the two hundred feet corresponding to the doubling of the area. Nobody can find this by means of arithmetic. For if we take fourteen, multiplication will give one hundred and ninety-six feet; if fifteen, two hundred and twenty-five feet. Therefore, since this

*trans. Morris Hicky Morgan, *Vitruvius, Ten Books on Architecture*, Harvard University Press, 1926.

is inexplicable by arithmetic, let a diagonal line be drawn from angle to angle of that square of ten feet in length and width, dividing it into two triangles of equal size, each fifty feet in area. Taking this diagonal line as the length, describe another square. Thus we shall have in the larger square four triangles of the same size and the same number of feet as the two of fifty feet each which were formed by the diagonal line in the smaller square. In this way Plato demonstrated the doubling by means of lines, as the figure appended at the bottom of the page will show.

Vitruvius's drawing has not survived. The square was not only used as a basis for the harmonious proportions of a cloister or to build pinnacles from a plan, but also in making the plans for certain churches. So the American archaeologist Sumner Crosby from Yale University, who organized a series of excavations at the abbey of Saint-Denis, reached the conclusion that the thirteenth-century architect conceived the reconstruction of the nave and the transept according to an *ad quadratum* plan. The following text, which is quoted in full, seems to present a particularly interesting problem with maximum clarity.

An attentive study of the nave and transepts proves that the plan of Pierre de Montreuil's constructions at Saint-Denis spring from it [an *ad quadratum* plan].

The geometrical problem of how to divide a square into nine equal squares and then subdivide the four corner squares into four still smaller squares each was resolved by the simplest means. Parallel lines dividing the sides of the square into three equal parts intercept diagonals at four principal points (the crossing), giving birth to nine equal squares. Perpendiculars dividing the corner squares in two divide each into four small squares. The solution is self-determining and is based strictly on intersections of 45° and 90°. Despite a certain number of irregularities, it is evident that this system was used at Saint-Denis to locate the placement of the transept piers. These irregularities appear only at those places where the new construction had to be joined to that of the twelfth century. A module* of 325 mm. must have been used. The 'royal' or 'Parisian' foot measured 324.84 mm. It is quickly realized that its use permitted the construction of a square that, with only the slightest corrections, matched the twelfth-century masonry and allowed the foundations of the nave which had been projected in the twelfth century to be used in the thirteenth for the new nave walls. This was the module which determined all of Pierre de Montreuil's major dimensions: the nave and transept bays are 6.50 m. long, or 20 modules, measured from the centre of one pier to another; the sides of the crossing measure 13 m., or 40 modules, as does the width of the nave, with a slight increase in width to the west so that it could be set on the twelfth-century foundations. Using the twelfth-century foundations caused the side aisles of the nave to be 7 m. wide, a deviation from the module. Another important dimension which seems to have been calculated on the module in accord with the general proportions of the transept was the height of the nave keystones which has been estimated as 29 m. But in point of fact, the distance from the pavement to immediately under the keystones of the ogives is 26 m. It is obviously difficult to determine with what scale the master of the works calculated the heights of the main vaults. And it must be remembered that the present level of the pavement is only approximately where it was in the thirteenth century. But, accepting the 26 m. measurement, the total is exactly 80 modules, which means that the proportion of the nave width to its height is 1 : 2 . . . The impeccable logic which resulted from the use of simple geometric principles produced harmonious proportions.**

The historical account of the duplication of the square, the Regensburg statute and Roriczer's book should not obscure Étienne Boileau's famous passage, nor the passages from the English Regius and Cooke manuscripts, all of which imply the existence of masons' secrets. In fact, paragraph 7 of Étienne Boileau's forty-eighth statute for masons, stonecutters, plasterers and mortar-makers

---

*A module is a variable unit of length used to serve as a basis for the planning measurements of a building.

**Sumner McKay Crosby, *The Abbey of St-Denis, 475-1122,* Yale University Press, 1942.

reads as follows: 'Masons, mortar-makers and plasterers may have as many assistants and valets as they please to help them in their work, provided they teach them nothing about their trade.'

It has been rightly noted that this is the only one of the 101 statutes registered by Étienne Boileau which includes a reference to a secret. It has been thought that such a text was peculiar to the building trade. This is not the case, since there are in England statutes for trades which have nothing to do with building which include paragraphs concerning discretion with regard to outsiders.

It must be pointed out that the relevant paragraph is addressed not to the overseers or stonecutters but to the humbler workmen like masons, mortar-makers and plasterers. The guild master was certainly not asking his workmen to conceal from their assistants such complicated techniques as the building of a pinnacle from a plan, for the simple reason that these workmen did not know enough to be able to understand the geometry of such complicated plans.

Presumably the guild master was asking his men not to reveal, for instance, the proportions of the ingredients needed to make mortar or plaster, or how to recognize the grain of the stone. This paragraph refers to tricks of the trade rather than to genuine secrets. The word 'secret' is, indeed, inappropriate here. In fact this famous paragraph can only really be understood in the context of the forty-eighth statute; it fits in with the royal wish and the guild master's wish to control a trade which, until then, had developed freely.

The two English manuscripts mentioned above are the Regius, written around 1390, and the Cooke, from about 1430. They have much in common, since they both take their inspiration from a manuscript drawn up in about 1360 which includes an exposé of the customs of masons and a legendary history of the trade. The Regius manuscript was drawn up by a clerk who was particularly interested in religion and moral precepts, and the Cooke manuscript by a man passionately interested in the trade. These two manuscripts do not lay down professional statutes like Étienne Boileau's or like the fourteenth-century London statutes, although they have some points in common with these. Throughout the centuries they have been recopied with many variations and they make up what are called masonic 'constitutions'. They played an important part in linking operative and speculative freemasonry. The customs are divided into two sections: 'Articles', which are addressed to the masters, and 'Points', which are addressed to the workmen. The latter must love God and the Church, accept money with humility, they must not quarrel and, finally, they must be discreet. The Cooke manuscript calls for discretion as follows: 'The third point is [the worker] keep secret the counsels of his fellows, whether given in the lodge, in the chamber, or any other place where masons be.'

Here are more precise instructions from the Regius manuscript: 'The third point must be stressed with the apprentice, therefore know it well. He keeps and guards his master's teachings and those of his fellows. He tells no man what he learns in the privacy of his chamber, nor does he reveal anything which he sees

Master John of Gloucester, who worked on Westminster Abbey.

Believed to be Henry of Reyns, first architect of Westminster Abbey.

or hears in the lodge or anything which happens there. Disclose to no man, no matter where you go, the discussions held in the hall or in the dormitory; keep them well, for your greatest honour, lest in being free with them you bring reproach upon yourself and great shame upon your profession.'

Masonic historians have long thought that these secrets which the workmen were asked to keep were of an esoteric nature. They were nothing of the sort, and we accept the opinions of D. Knoop and G.P. Jones, who wrote: 'It is well known that there were "secrets" because the Articles and Points forbid their revelation; but there is no reason to suppose that these secrets contained anything more esoteric than the remarks or discussions in the lodge (which did not need to be told to employers) as well as technical secrets of the trade concerning, for example, the design of an arch or the manner of placing a stone so that as much of its grain as possible followed the position it had had in the quarry bed.'

Any discussion of the secret is incomplete without reference to the origins of the signs by which freemasons recognize each other today. French or English cathedral builders had no need of special handshakes or secret signs in order to recognize each other. According to D. Knoop and G.P. Jones this practice began in Scotland. Particular conditions pertaining to stonemasonry led highly qualified workers to adopt secret ways of introducing themselves. These conditions were, on the one hand, the existence of the 'entered apprentice', who was to be found nowhere else, and the absence of freestone in Scotland. Workers capable of cutting this particular stone were unable to prove their skill and had to contend with competition from barely qualified men, the cowans, who originally built dry stone walls. In order to prevent the cowans from being employed to do work for which they were not qualified, the stonecutters decided to adopt secret signs of recognition among themselves.

The 1707 document of the Mother Kilwinning lodge supports this theory: 'No mason may employ a cowan without the password . . .' These signs of recognition, which were known to exist in operative freemasonry in the sixteenth century, must have been adopted in seventeenth-century Scotland in the early days of speculative freemasonry. This custom then spread from Scotland to England while, on the other hand, masonic constitutions spread from England to Scotland, where they had initially been unknown.

Thanks to numerous archives and to inscriptions engraved in stone, the names of many of the great thirteenth-century cathedral builders survive. The text from the labyrinth at Amiens was quoted earlier (see p. 41). It included the names of three architects who between 1220 and 1288 succeeded one another in supervising the building of the cathedral: Robert de Luzarches, Thomas de Cormont and his son, Regnault.

The inscription in the labyrinth at Rheims tells us that the chevet which was begun in 1211 was the work of Jean d'Orbais; work was continued by Jean Le

Photogram of rose window.

Façade of Strasbourg Cathedral as it stands today.

Loup and Gaucher de Rheims. The façade with the great rose window was by Bernard de Soissons, who worked on it for about thirty-five years, from 1255 to 1290. This Bernard de Soissons must have been quite wealthy, because a 1287 register of the *taille* levied to pay the expenses of Philip the Fair's coronation records that he was taxed in two parishes. He paid 5 sous in Saint-Denis and a further 100 in Saint-Symphorien.

Also in Rheims, the name survives of the very talented architect of the beautiful church of Saint-Nicaise, which has unfortunately been destroyed. Like many architects, he was honoured by being buried in the church he had built. The tombstone reads: 'Here lies Maître Hue Libergié who began this church in the year 1229 and who departed this life in the year 1267.' Today the tombstone can be seen in the cathedral with Hue Libergié dressed in a long robe and surrounded by the tools of his profession – a set square, a compass and a graduated rule.

A particularly famous tombstone commemorates in glowing terms the architect Pierre de Montreuil, who was in charge of the building site of Notre-Dame de Paris, *c.* 1260-65. He also built the refectory and the Lady chapel of the monastery of Saint-Germain-des-Prés, where he was buried. His epitaph reads: 'Here lies Pierre de Montreuil, perfect flower of good morality, in his lifetime doctor of stonework, may the King of Heaven lead him to celestial heights.' (Note the academic title of 'doctor' of stonework.) His reputation was so great, even after his death, that his wife had the honour of being buried beside him in the chapel. This is also evidence of the respect in which women, even from humble origins, were held at the time: 'Here lies Anne, formerly wife of the late Maître Pierre de Montreuil. Pray God for her soul.'

Yet another epitaph glorifies the memory of the architect of the thirteenth-century choir of the abbey of Saint-Étienne in Caen: 'Here lies Guillaume, distinguished in the art of stonework, who completed this new work.' But, without doubt, the most surprising inscription is engraved, eight metres long, on the base of the south transept in Notre-Dame de Paris. It tells us who built the transept: 'Maître Jean de Chelles began this work on the second day of the ides of February 1258.' What nineteenth- or twentieth-century architect has ever been honoured by having his name inscribed in such a remarkable manner on the building which he designed? In England, for instance, the Royal Institute of British Architects allows its members to inscribe their names on their buildings only in letters that are no more than two inches high.

We should remember that all these inscriptions date from the second part of the thirteenth century, when the architect perhaps became fully aware of his own importance. The thirteenth century probably witnessed a complete transformation in his role: he no longer worked manually and he came to be treated differently from the workmen. The preacher Nicolas de Biard bore witness to this evolution in the middle of the century; he was shocked to see the architect no longer working with his hands. 'In these large buildings,' he exclaimed, 'there is habitually a master who merely gives orders and never puts his hand to work and yet he receives more money than the others . . . The master masons carry gloves and a stick and say to the others "Cut it this way", and they don't work and still they are given a greater reward; and this is the way with many modern prelates.'

Such was their prestige at the time that architects were allowed to have stone busts of themselves placed in the churches which they had built. Above the stone bust of Mathieu d'Arras in the triforium of the choir in Prague Cathedral an inscription reads: 'Mathieu, native of the city of Arras in France, first master of the works of this church. Charles IV, then Margrave of Moravia, brought him from Avignon to build this church which Mathieu began from the foundations in the year 1344 and the building of which he supervised until 1352 when he died.' In those days France exported architects as nowadays she exports engineers. The bust of Peter Parler, who succeeded Mathieu d'Arras at Prague, has been placed beside the busts of the princely benefactors of the cathedral.

The word 'magister' preceding the words 'cementarius' and 'lathomus' sometimes, although not always, designates an architect. This word 'magister' or master has also been borrowed by the mechanical arts from the liberal arts. Originally 'magister' described those who had completed a course in the liberal arts. Thirteenth-century doctors of law were annoyed because carpenters had assumed this honorary title without having any right to it. The expression 'magister operis', master of the works, unlike the word 'architect', does not designate a profession. In England the master of the works was very often an official nominated by the King to supervise work in progress. 'Magister operis' may on the other hand designate an architect.

The architect drew up the plans and this he did in the tracing house which was a room set aside for the purpose. The tracing-house floor was covered in plaster on which the architect drew in life size part of a vault or of some other feature of the church, indicating every possible aspect of it. The carpenters were then called for, and they, using special planks, cut out templates from which the stone was then shaped.

The architect was assisted on the large sites by an 'overseer' or foreman, whom the Germans called 'parlier' because his role was to talk to the workmen. It was often he who drew the plans with his large compass. The foreman and the architect have, in fact, sometimes been confused, and some medieval illustrations have portrayed the architect holding one of these large compasses.

A tracing house survives to this day, above the chapter house at York Minster, its floor covered with architectural drawings. One drawing of a window is said to be by Master William Hoton; this window is supposed to have been built in about 1395 by Hugh Hedor and it can be seen in the choir of the Minster. Nineteenth-century wood and zinc panels now hang on the walls of the tracing house.

Top: Mathieu d'Arras, the first architect of Prague Cathedral. *Bottom:* Peter Parler, the second architect of Prague Cathedral.

Master Humbert, architect of the collegiate church of Saint-Martin de Colmar, south doorway (end thirteenth century).

Drawings not unlike the ones in York can be found on the paving stones of several French cathedrals, notably Limoges, Clermont and Narbonne. There are others which often remain unnoticed in various parish churches. In the fourteenth-century church at Ménerbes in the Vaucluse, a whole series of architectural drawings is engraved on a wall of one of the chapels.

No plaster or wood models seem to have been made by architects throughout the whole 'cathedral crusade'. This method used in classical antiquity to represent buildings in three dimensions seems to have survived for some time during the early Middle Ages only to disappear for several centuries and to reappear in the Renaissance.

Unhappily, few architectural drawings survive from the ascendant era of the Middle Ages. Villard de Honnecourt's sketchbook includes elevations, but these drawings were meant as inspiration for future works rather than as actual plans. Villard drew ground plans of three churches: the abbey of Vaucelles, Notre-Dame de Cambrai and the cathedral at Meaux.

How can the absence of such basic documents as plans be explained? It must be realized that there was no particular reason to keep plans of completed buildings – indeed it is difficult enough to obtain the plans of large buildings which were put up at the beginning of this century. No importance was attached to their preservation. On the other hand, these plans must often have been drawn on plaster or on wooden boards. The price of parchment was prohibitive. Is it by chance that so. many fourteenth- and fifteenth-century plans on parchment survive? Probably not, since the price of this material had fallen by then.

The best-known thirteenth-century drawings are the Rheims Palimpsest and the plans for Strasbourg Cathedral. In 1838 original drawings dating from about 1250 were found in a manuscript belonging to the cathedral chapter at Rheims. The drawings were plans for buildings and were half covered by drawings dating from no later than 1270. Parchment was expensive and therefore had to be used over again. One of the plans which can be deciphered beneath the more recent drawing shows the elevation of a large church. This drawing, which John Harvey claims to be attributable to Hue Libergié or one of his collaborators, is remarkable in that the artist drew a median line through the middle of the façade. He then made a detailed plan of the left-hand side of the façade but only made a rough outline of the right-hand side.

A very interesting series of drawings survies in the *maison de l'œuvre* at Strasbourg. The first one, (A), shows what may have been the first plan for the cathedral and must date from around 1275. The second drawing, (A *bis*), would appear to be a copy of the first one with added decorative elements which were incorporated in the façade built in about 1300.

A detailed estimate like the one drawn up in 1284 for the rebuilding of the Cordeliers' church at Provins serves as a useful complement to the plans. It has

Drawing (*c. 1275*) of plan A for Strasbourg Cathedral: elevation of the southern half of the west façade.

Plan A *bis*, copy of plan A with addition of
decorative elements.

been pointed out that measurements were only rarely specified on medieval
plans. The following extracts from this estimate show that some measurements
were given in feet.

In the name of the Father, the Son and the Holy Spirit, Amen. This is the
estimate for the convent of the Frères Mineurs at Provins. Firstly the convent
shall be razed to the ground. The front gable and the side will be the same size
they were before but the side of the wing will be built on round pillars with
arches the same length as the old wing. The height of the curve of these arches
will be determined by their width to allow them to join the entablature which
will support the structure of the nave; and there will be, on this side, as many
arches as there will be bays between the tie-beams, all dictated by the length of
the old wing; and the size of the arches will be governed by the structure. On the
courtyard side, where the springing line meets the gable, there will be a
six-foot-deep buttress with a three-foot bond-stone, which will be cushioned by
a chamfered facing above the support of the gable.

Nicolas de Biard was right when he claimed that the principal master was paid considerably more than the others; but he should not have been indignant, since it is only to be expected that men who can direct a site and draw up plans and estimates should be socially superior to and financially better off than masons and stonecutters. The chapters had to petition these exceptional men who between them were so full of moral qualities and so learned in technical knowledge. The number of men with these qualities and this knowledge was, after all, fairly limited.

An attempt was made to retain architects under advantageous contracts. They were asked to swear not to work on other sites while their contracts lasted. But they did not always accept this restriction of their liberty, and obviously they took advantage of their privileged position in order to dictate their terms of employment. The most amusing example of this – because of its relevance now – was the contract which the architect Raymond demanded of the Archbishop of Lugo in 1129. Pierre du Colombier points out that in his contract, Raymond, making allowances for a possible fall in the value of money during his employment as master of the cathedral works, asked to be paid mainly in kind – more precisely, in 6 silver marks, 36 metres of cloth, 17 loads of wood and as many pairs of shoes and gaiters as he would need per month, 2 sous for food, 1 measure of salt and a pound of candles.

Architects could be employed for a year, for as long as the site was open, or, in exceptional cases, for life. In the latter case provision was made for some kind of a pension in case of sickness. Materially, they had many advantages, including, as often as not, free lodging. They were given clothes and sometimes furs and might be exempt from tax. In addition to all this, they often received a lump sum on a certain date every year. They also earned extra money from giving their expert advice. When there was a fire or when a vault collapsed, the chapter often decided to call a meeting of some of the most respected architects before rebuilding began. These experts came to examine the damage and then together they drew up a list of their conclusions. The chapter, having lodged and fed them suitably, gave them sums of money which in the terms of their annual wage were quite considerable.

Thanks to their contracts and the valuations they gave, architects became quite rich and could buy their own houses – it has been pointed out that Bernard de Soissons owned two houses in Rheims. They sometimes acquired quarries and sold stone to the cathedral site where they worked. Little by little, some of them were able to set themselves up as independent contractors, although they could only undertake small works. Contracts for these modest sites were, as they would be today, granted to the lowest bidder.

Henry III, so as to cut the considerable costs of Westminster Abbey, decided to order his master of the works to have some jobs put out to tender. In May 1253 the abbey accounts report: 'For the contract for the chapter house door, 25 pounds. For the chapel contract, 9 pounds.'

Life's vagaries led some of these architects to become town-planners and thus they designed new towns. They drew circular towns like Bram in the Languedoc or square ones like Aigues-Mortes. Some specialized in fortified castles and others in building bridges. The legend of the *frères pontifes*, who travelled from one town to another building bridges, is quite romantic but has no bearing on reality. There are agreements concerning the building of bridges in many archives, but none of them mentions the activities of these brethren.

Towards the middle of the eleventh century Pons, the abbot of Aniane, signed an agreement with Geffroi, the abbot of Saint-Guilhem-du-Désert for a bridge to be built over the Hérault. The former undertook to provide transport for all the wood, stone, lime, sand, iron and lead and to supply the ropes. The latter agreed to build half the bridge at the monastery's expense and to pay the master of the works.

At Arles on 15 June 1178, forty-one days before the coronation of the Emperor Frederick in the same town, a settlement was reached between Jean de Manduel and the people of Arles on the one hand and the Jews on the other hand. The latter were committed to a hundred years of forced labour, which involved building, to be done every Holy Saturday. The forced labour was to be replaced by a payment of 50 sous and a future annual tax of 20 sous.

The truth about the legend of the bridge-building brethren is that brotherhoods really were formed independently of each other in different towns. Their job was to look after pilgrims and to supervise the upkeep of bridges and the payment of tolls. The Pont-Saint-Esprit brotherhood, for instance, existed until as late as 1794.

The Builder Monks

In some respects monastery building differed considerably from cathedral building – in, for instance, the management of sites, labour and the choice of plans. However, the building of monasteries was an important manifestation of the medieval creative genius and closely related to cathedral building. Since monastic archives are particularly rich, discussion of the subject will highlight the characteristics of the cathedral builders and clarify certain aspects of organization common to all types of religious building.

Gervais, a Benedictine monk from Canterbury, left an informative detailed account of the reconstruction of the cathedral choir after the 1174 fire. Thanks to this document we can envisage life on a monastery site in the twelfth century.

Wishing to repair the damage as soon as possible, the monks called in experts for advice: 'French and English craftsmen were therefore summoned, but even these differed in opinion. Some undertook to repair the columns without mischief to the walls above. On the other hand there were some who asserted that the whole church must be pulled down if the monks wished to be safe. This opinion, true as it was, tormented the monks with grief.'

It will be noted that there were no 'builders' in the community. The monks hired a French architect, William of Sens, who, like Villard de Honnecourt in the next century, was an expert in stonework and carpentry.

Among the other workmen there had come a certain William of Sens, a man active and ready and as a craftsman most skilful in both wood and stone. Him therefore they retained, on account of his lively genius and good reputation, and dismissed the others . . . And he, . . . carefully surveying the burnt walls in their upper and lower parts, within and without, did for a time yet conceal what he found necessary to be done, lest the truth should kill them in their present state of faint-heartedness. But he went on preparing all things that were needful for the work, either of himself or by the agency of others. And when he found that the monks began to be somewhat comforted, he ventured to confess that the pillars rent with fire and all that they supported must be destroyed if the monks

Fontenay Abbey in the Côte d'Or.

wished to have a safe and excellent building. At length . . . they consented, patiently if not willingly, to the destruction of the choir.

When the monks admitted to the necessity of razing the old choir, William of Sens could at last set about acquiring the stone needed for the rebuilding 'from beyond sea'. And the stone, with which he was certainly familiar and which was one of the best stones known to the Middle Ages, came from Caen. This stone is still valued today in England and was used on a site in the City of London in 1955. Whilst awaiting the stone, William turned his hand to engineering. 'He constructed ingenious machines for loading and unloading ships, and for lifting masonry and stones.' So Villard de Honnecourt was no exception; medieval architects were more or less obliged to be engineers too. Meanwhile William of Sens was also busy supplying the stonecutters with templates.

Whilst preparations for the rebuilding of the church were in progress, the old choir was demolished. This dangerous job was usually entrusted to specialists (called pickmen) who are rarely mentioned in the archives. The choir was demolished and nothing else was done that year. Gervais takes up the story of the reconstruction year by year:

The master began . . . to prepare all things necessary for the new work and to destroy the old. In this way the first year was taken up. In the following year, after the feast of St Bertin [5 September 1175] before the winter, he erected four pillars, that is, two on each side; and after the winter two more were placed, so that on each side were three in order, upon which and upon the exterior walls of the aisles he framed seemly arches and a vault . . . With these works the second year was occupied.

In the third year he placed two pillars on each side . . . In the summer of the fourth year, beginning from the crossing, he erected ten pillars, that is, five on each side . . . He was, at the beginning of the fifth year, in the act of preparing with machines for the turning of the great vault, when suddenly the beams broke under his feet and he fell to the ground, stones and timbers accompanying his fall, from the height of the capitals of the upper vault, that is to say fifty feet.

He was injured and had to take to his bed, but his health did not improve. This accident shows that during the second half of the twelfth century architects were still very close to workmen. They physically took part in the building, and Nicolas de Biard could not have talked about them as he did about his contemporaries in the middle of the next century.

As the winter approached and it was necessary to finish the upper vault, he gave charge of the work to a certain ingenious and industrious monk, who was the overseer of the masons; an appointment whence much envy and malice arose, as it made the young man appear more skilful than those of higher rank and position. But the master lying in bed commanded all things should be done in

Accidents on building sites. (Moralizing Bible, Vienna, mid-thirteenth century and manuscript from the Escorial.)

order. And thus was completed the ciborium between the four principal pillars
. . . Two ciboria on each side were formed before the winter, when heavy rains
beginning stopped the work. In these operations the fourth year was occupied
and the beginning of the fifth.

The master, perceiving that he gained no benefit from the physicians, gave up
the work and returned to his home in France. And another succeeded him, in
charge of the works: William by name, English by nation, small in body, but in
workmanship of many kinds acute and honest.

The technical knowledge the young monk had gained during the few years
when he had been in close contact with the builders was clearly not enough for
him to be able to supervise the work single-handed after William of Sens's
departure. Unfortunately, monasteries never had schools for stonecutters or
architects, which would have made it possible for the monks to build their
monasteries with no outside help.

He, in the summer of the fifth year, finished the transept on each side, and
turned the ciborium which is above the high altar, which the rains of the
previous year had hindered, although all was prepared. Moreover, he laid the
foundation for the enlargement of the church at the east end, where a chapel of
St Thomas was to be built . . . Having formed a most substantial foundation for
the exterior wall with stone and cement, he erected the wall of the crypt as high
as the bases of the windows. Thus was the fifth year employed and the
beginning of the sixth.

In the beginning of the sixth year from the fire, when the works were
resumed, the monks were seized with a violent longing to prepare the choir, so
that they might enter it at the coming Easter. And the master set himself
manfully to work to satisfy the wishes of the convent . . . So the monks . . .
returned into the new choir in 1180, on 19 April, at about the ninth hour of Easter
Eve.

The seventh year from the fire . . . included the completion of the new and
handsome crypt, and above the crypt the exterior walls of the walls of the aisles
up to thin marble capitals . . . In this eighth year the master erected eight interior
pillars and turned the arches and the vault with the windows in the circuit. He
also raised the tower up to the bases of the highest windows under the vault. In
the ninth year no work was done, for want of funds. In the tenth year the upper
windows of the tower, together with the vault, were finished . . . The tower was
covered in and many other things done this year (1184).*

If such a rich and powerful monastery as Canterbury lacked funds so that for
a whole year workmen could not be paid nor raw materials bought, it is easy to

* Gervais's account is taken from Professor Willis's translation in his *Architectural History of
Canterbury Cathedral* and quoted also in L. F. Salzman, *Building in England down to 1540*,
Clarendon Press, 1952.

Looking up into the vaulting: St. Philibert
                                                de Tournus.

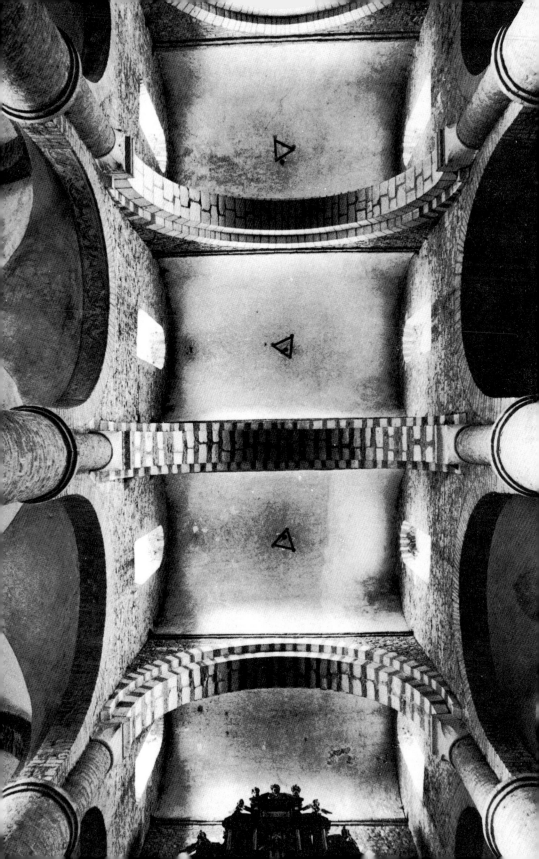

understand why it sometimes took several centuries to build lesser monasteries, parish churches and cathedrals.

It will be noted that, with one exception, the monks do not appear to have participated in the rebuilding of their choir. This is not altogether surprising. Several decades ago now, in England, G.G. Coulton cast doubt on the active part played by monks as builders. His thesis, which gave rise to passionate discussions in the national press, accused Montalembert of having originated what he called the legend of the builder monks in his nineteenth-century work, *Les Moines d'Occident*. Coulton's followers pursued the polemic for some time. Today the heat has abated and it is easier to see things more clearly. But it must be recognized that this problem is one of the most complex of medieval architecture.

A quotation from Orderic Vital, who wrote in the first half of the twelfth century, supports Montalembert's thesis: 'All Cistercian monasteries are built in isolated spots in the middle of woods and the monks build them with their own hands.' This sentence calls for two important comments. First, Orderic Vital says the Cistercians, and not the Benedictines, built their own monasteries and, secondly, in the Cistercian order, the word 'réligieux' which he uses describes priests and lay brothers. The history of monastery building, in fact, requires certain distinctions to be made: on the one hand are the Benedictines, on the other the Cistercians; and in Cistercian monasteries there was a difference between the building activities of priests and of lay brothers.

To understand these differences it is necessary to refer to source material and read the Rule of St Benedict. The Rule says absolutely nothing about building. The monk's purpose is to devote his life to God through meditation, prayer and the mass; the life of the order is organized to do God's work. Manual labour is only encouraged in so far as it contributes towards this. Manual labour must only be done 'in a limited way because of the weak'. Harvesting, which is an arduous task, should only be done in exceptional cases. The order encourages work like gardening or jobs done in a workshop. The spirit of the Rule does not allow for the hard work of a quarryman, a stonecutter or a sculptor.

The Benedictine historian Ursmer Berlière confirms this when he writes that the monastic order, which by reason of its constitution postulates a life of solitude, could not lend itself in anything but a limited fashion to heavy agricultural or manual labour, and he goes so far as to add that the limited amount of manual work was reduced or even disappeared as members of the order were promoted to the priesthood. (Monks were not priests in St Benedict's days.)

As the importance of monasteries increased both economically and socially, gardening and manual work like household duties were done by servants (*famuli, canonici, matricularii, ministeriales*), who often made up a large part of the population of big monasteries. This gave useful and favourable positions to numerous freemen and serfs. In the eleventh century reformers in Southern Germany and in Italy had the idea of making these laymen into monks, and they became lay brothers. This solution had the advantage of preventing the monks from having too many contacts with the outside world, contacts which might harm contemplation and the spiritual life. The idea of a religious body of labourers was taken up and codified by the Cistercians, who published in 1119 the 'usages and customs' of the lay brothers. Henceforth there were to be two categories of monks: priests, who could particularly devote themselves to a spiritual and intellectual life, and the lay brothers, to whom practical tasks were given. The latter had to take a vow of poverty, chastity and obedience, but could never become priests. They had their own refectory and dormitories. They were gardeners, cobblers, tailors, tanners, smiths and masons. Thanks to these lay brothers, the part played by Cistercians in the building of their monasteries was real indeed; but the history of the rebuilding of Clairvaux and the stonecutters' marks on the walls of Cistercian buildings prove that builders were called in from outside.

It is of interest to study the building of a twentieth-century monastery in order to understand some of the problems of the past. Nowadays the Benedictines have adopted the Cistercian principle of the lay brothers. At the beginning of the century the Benedictine monks at Buckfast Abbey in Devon discovered twelfth-century Cistercian foundations and decided to rebuild their church. There being no 'builder' among the lay brothers, the Father Abbot sent a young monk, Brother Peter, to En Calcat in France, to learn the rudiments of masonry from the specialized men who were engaged in rebuilding that abbey. He came back to England after eighteen months and worked on the site day after day for thirty-two years. The work was often very arduous and his hands were burnt by lime – making it clear, incidentally, why site overseers in the Middle Ages regularly bought gloves for the masons.

Brother Peter taught the rudiments which he had learnt at En Calcat to four or five other lay brothers. The work required of them was above all mixing mortar, masonry, and, in exceptional cases, stonecutting, which required a longer apprenticeship. (As soon as there was enough money, ready-cut stones were bought from the quarry.) The Father Abbot, in conformity with the lay brothers' 'usages and customs', exempted them from some holy offices; they had only to attend the first one in the morning and compline in the evening. They could thus work uninterruptedly from morning to night.

The number of lay brothers whom the Father Abbot could put to work on the site was limited by monastic life itself. If too many lay brothers were building, the regularity of life in the monastery might be disturbed, and this regularity was essential to contemplation and the service of God. It seems that for the well-being of a Benedictine community a third of the monks needed to be lay. Figures published by the papacy in 1935 indicated that 33% of some 10,000

Benedictines were lay brothers. The problem of recruiting them is as acute in prosperous Western countries today as it was in Western Europe at the end of the thirteenth century.

None of the monks at Buckfast Abbey had studied architecture before joining the order, although this was not the case in other monasteries. An outside architect, Frederick Walters, was asked to draw up the plans and supervise the building; and a volunteer monk was called for by the Father Abbot to supervise the lay brothers. The monk who agreed to become the Father Builder was Father Richard, and his physical efforts over the years cost him dearly. He was not dispensed from attending morning service.

As soon as it became known that the monks at Buckfast were rebuilding their church, gifts came pouring in, and so the work could be speeded up. The framework and the roofing were done by outside specialists. Generous benefactors donated the gold high altar, the Stations of the Cross and the choirstalls. Meanwhile the monks themselves were far from idle. Some of the fathers, like the Abbey historian, Dom John Stephen, continued with their research; others, like Dom Norris, planned the vast frescoes which now adorn the ceiling of the Lantern Tower. The church was completed in 1936.

The rebuilding of the Landévennec monastery in the extreme west of Brittany, which was put in hand in 1950, initially depended substantially on voluntary labour. The Bishop of Quimper wrote a pastoral letter announcing Father Abbot Kerbénéat's plans to rebuild Landévennec Abbey. He asked people to lodge the priests passing through their parishes. In their turn the parish priests proclaimed the Benedictines' plans from the pulpit, and asked for volunteers to help the monks reclaim and level the land at Landévennec to prepare for the building. Such was the faith of the Breton people that groups of agricultural workers left their homes and came forward throughout the winter, from December to February, to answer the appeal. Groups of twenty to fifty parishioners would set out with their tools before dawn in order to reach Landévennec by sunrise, and they returned to their villages at nightfall. Their help was particularly appreciated at Landévennec at a time when the monks did not have sufficient funds to employ a work force. Voluntary work has been estimated there at around 1,200 days.

In addition to his appeal for voluntary labour and with the help of the towns and villages in the diocese, the Father Abbot organized a large bazaar in which the population participated keenly. The funds thus raised were used to employ a contractor from Landernau for the building of the abbey itself. Barely eight years later, in 1958, the Kerbénéat monks could, thanks to the active support of the Breton people, return to the venerable site at Landévennec.

Lay brothers building Buckfast Abbey.

Engineers and Technicians

The history of technology is a recent discipline and few historians have studied in any depth the fascinating questions which arise from it. The history of science has been studied more closely, but it is quite different and has less bearing on the past. Few societies were aware of science, whereas technology has, without exception, always been in evidence. Specifically, the history of technology shows that the cathedral builders played an active part in the first European industrial revolution. More generally, it suggests that invention seems to be regulated by certain laws. Invention is favoured, for instance, in periods of ascendancy in a society, when the society is intellectually very alive and is shaping its ideals. When the society reaches maturity and change and new technology may threaten its prosperity, the fervour for invention subsides.

Energy has always been the basis of a country's industrial power. In the Middle Ages the three main sources of energy were water, wind and the horse, with hydraulic power as essential to economic life as oil is to us today. The development of the water mill during the early Middle Ages resulted partly from the broader network of regularly flowing rivers and streams to be found in the northern regions, and partly, in the tenth century, from a vastly increased population. The water mill was known in Asia Minor in the first century B.C., but for climatic and hydrological reasons it was not developed around the Mediterranean basin – the heart of classical civilization. The mills at Barbegal in Provence, which cost so much to operate, demonstrate the difficulties which confronted the Romans in their attempts to utilize water power. Yet in 1086 William the Conqueror recorded 5,624 water mills in England. By the thirteenth century there were some tens of thousands in France. Enormous works were undertaken in the towns to dig diversion canals for these mills. In the countryside all the rivers were used. The advantage of this source of energy was that it could be found everywhere.

In Toulouse, in spite of a rapid and frequently dangerous current, engineers managed to build an immense 300-metre causeway blocking the river diagonally in order to create a fall of water which would be powerful enough to drive the mills at Bazacle. An enormous sum of money was needed to build this causeway

The rigid padded collar enabled the horse to play an important role in the economic expansion of the Middle Ages. (Bibliothèque de Genève.)

and to carry out such a gigantic scheme. The more enterprising citizens created a joint stock company. Each member had a share in profits or losses of the company according to his holding.

The inclusion of water mills in the system of feudal rights meant the end of manually operated mills. By the use of the camshaft, the circular movement could be replaced by a reciprocating movement, and so hydraulic energy could be used not only to grind grain, but to pull cloth, to make beer, to powder oak bark for tanning, to forge iron and to make paper. Then, as now, a lever was all that was needed to set the machinery in motion. It seems inconceivable that the word 'artisan' should be used to describe the men who made and used these machines and who thereby put an end to a considerable amount of manual labour.

From the twelfth century, not only were innumerable windmills built to take advantage of the wind as a source of energy, but mills driven by the tide were also built. In this field the Middle Ages heralded L'Electricité de France on La Rance.

The horse, too, because of the part it played in land reclamation and in carrying materials to the sites, contributed to the boom in the Western world. Horses were used a great deal on the cathedral sites. For the first time in history, due to a series of inventions, the horse's maximum strength was put to the test. Horseshoes were invented to protect the animals' hooves, the old Roman roads were replaced by roads with better paving. Harnessing was altered and horses no longer took the weight of a load on a strap around the neck but on a shoulder collar, which meant that their strength could be used to greater advantage. Furthermore, they could be hitched up to form teams, one behind the other, and more often than not they replaced oxen, which were slower and less manageable.

Alongside these sources of energy, human activities developed. Advances were made in weaving, the spinning wheel was invented, iron was made harder. Lathes were improved and the mechanical clock was invented. The experimental method in agriculture was used and artesian wells were dug. There was intensified rearing of livestock and vineyards were improved, the compass and the stern rudder were introduced. Chimneys were built, coal burnt, wax candles were used for lighting, forks, spectacles and mirrors appeared, and paper was made.

Documents prove that at the time there was an awareness of the advantages of technology. The writer of a Cistercian report remarks that the disciplined use of the forces of nature relieved the labourer of some hard work which became mechanized. The Franciscan monk Bartholomew understood the importance of iron, not only for use in war, but in agriculture and in building. 'From many points of view,' he wrote in 1260, 'iron is more useful to man than gold, although greedy souls covet gold more than iron. Without iron men could neither defend

Builders at work, showing treadwheels for raising materials. (Wenzel Bible, fourteenth century.)

themselves against their enemies nor impose the law; the innocent ensure the defeat of their enemies and the impudence of the wicked is punished thanks to iron. Equally, all manual labour requires iron without which the land could not be cultivated, nor houses built.'

This technological boom was only made possible because medieval society believed in progress and men were not blinded by tradition. The past could and

Tools for stone work and slate.

should be improved upon. Gilbert de Tournai said: 'Never will we find the truth if we allow ourselves to be satisfied with what has already been discovered . . . those who wrote before our time were not lords, but guides. The truth is available to all men and it has not yet been fully discovered.'

Emile Bréhier in his *Philosophie du Moyen Age* wrote that this freedom from past authorities, which was expressed by the specific and reasoned choice of a thesis, was linked to a belief in the possibility of progress – manifested for the first time in the Middle Ages. John of Salisbury quoted Abélard's statement that a modern man could compose a dialectic in no way inferior to the ancients', and added that Bernard (Master of the episcopal school at Chartres from 1114 to 1119) used to say: 'We are as dwarfs mounted on the shoulders of giants, so that we can perceive much more than they, not because our vision is clearer, nor because we are taller but because we are lifted higher thanks to their gigantic height.'

The cathedral builders, in a society which believed in progress, were able to innovate, and the cathedrals built at the end of the thirteenth century result from hundreds of innovations and improvements created by the builders' spirit of discovery. Most crafts progressed side by side, and often advances in the one helped the other. For instance, the progress made by smiths helped architects, sculptors and stonecutters. These smiths were cathedral builders in so far as they made stronger steel tools, which in their turn could cut harder stone like the stone at Volvic near Clermont. Previously this had been impossible to cut. Besides, sculptors were then able to work the stone more delicately, and the use of harder stone led architects to design slenderer columns and thinner walls.

Being harder, tools needed less sharpening. A smith's team would be made up of a smith, an assistant, an axe-bearer, a labourer to take the tools to and from the sharpener, and another workman to stoke the forge with charcoal. Unfortunately, little is known of the origins and social position of these men who were in a group apart from the other builders. There was a forge on every site and at every quarry. At Autun about 10% of expenses went towards the forge: 'To the forge at Autun for the year, 42 pounds, 10 sous, 6 deniers . . . To the quarry forge 3 pounds, 2 sous.'

Smiths not only made tools, iron claws (for lifting heavy stones), all types of nails, horseshoes and tie-rods, like those used in Westminster Abbey to prevent the walls from separating, but also iron chains, which architects decided to have sealed inside the walls for reinforcement. The architect of the Sainte Chapelle, for instance, is known to have had chains built into the walls. But the experiment was not entirely satisfactory because of damage to the stone, and in this instance we are confronted by a technical development which in the long run was not an advance.

The architect who designed the John Hancock Building in Boston used a new type of window which turned out to be unable to stand up to the wind. The circulation of air between the pane of glass and the metal frame in fact caused a series of accidents in 1974. A catastrophe like the one at Beauvais in 1284, caused by technical mistakes, could occur also in the modern world. Yet the architects of the Gothic cathedrals, like Amiens, knew how to build their great churches so that the tallest parts could stand up to winds of around 90 mph.

Recently, by means of a technique used in industry, an American civil engineer, Robert Mark, studied the structure and wind resistance of medieval churches. A polarized light reveals the lines of force and the weak points on a plastic model of the building. Such an experiment makes it easier to understand how different parts of the building helped to support the whole. This technique has made it possible to understand the need for certain architectural elements, like, for instance, pinnacles, which had formerly often been seen as merely decorative.

Unlike stonecutting techniques, carpentry techniques were not lost during the early Middle Ages, but carpenters adapted their frameworks as vaulting developed and changed. The framework for the ribbed vaulting of a thirteenth-century cathedral is a marvel in itself and is the result of endless improvements in technique. The Franciscan monk Bartholomew was quite right to stress the importance of iron in the building of the day, for it was thanks to the smiths that greatly improved carpentry tools were available. This meant that timberwork, shoring and scaffolding were more reliable. The carpenters, too,

Spire of Notre-Dame de Paris; model built by 'compagnons charpentiers' in 1971.

Carpenters' marks on twelfth-century timber.

Young carpenter checking accuracy of working drawing.

were able to adapt to the particular conditions of their country and of their times – to such things as the lack of large pieces of timber. Villard de Honnecourt was concerned with this problem and explained how to build a tower, a house or a bridge from small pieces of wood: 'In this way you can work on a tower or a house with planks which are even too short . . . And by this method a bridge can be built across water with wood which is only 20 feet long.'

By the twelfth century it was already difficult to find large trees, as the forests had been devastated. With his usual enthusiasm, Suger tells how, despite the contrary advice of specialists, he found in the forest of Iveline, 'thanks to God and the Holy Martyrs,' some trees of vast diameter which were absolutely necessary for Saint-Denis.

When the work had been finished in great part, when the storeys of the old and new building had been joined, and when we had laid aside the anxiety we had long felt because of those gaping cracks in the old walls, we undertook with new confidence to repair the damages in the great capitals and in the bases that supported the columns. But when we inquired both of our own carpenters and those of Paris where we might find beams, we were told, as was in their opinion true, that such could in no wise be found in these regions owing to the lack of woods; they would inevitably have to be brought hither from the district of Auxerre. All concurred with this view and we were much distressed by this because of the magnitude of the task and the long delay of the work; but on a certain night, when I had returned from celebrating Matins, I began to think in bed that I myself should go through all the forests of these parts, look around everywhere and alleviate those delays and troubles if [beams] could be found here. Quickly disposing of other duties and hurrying in the early morning, we hastened with our carpenters, and with the measurements of the beams, to the forest called Iveline. When we traversed our possession in the Valley of Chevreuse we summoned through our servants the keepers of our own forests as well as men who knew about the other woods, and questioned them under oath whether we could find there, no matter with how much trouble, any timbers of that measure. At this they smiled, or rather would have laughed at us if they had dared; they wondered whether we were quite ignorant of the fact that nothing of the kind could be found in the entire region, especially since Milon, the Castellan of Chevreuse (our vassal, who holds of us one half of the forest in addition to another fief) had left nothing unimpaired or untouched that could be used for building palisades and bulwarks while he was long subjected to wars both by our Lord the King and Amaury de Montfort. We however – scorning whatever they might say – began, with the courage of our faith as it were, to search through the woods; and toward the first hour we found one timber adequate to the measure. Why say more? By the ninth hour or sooner we had, through the thickets, the depths of the forests and the dense, thorny tangles, marked down twelve timbers (for so many were necessary) to the astonishment of all, especially those on the spot; and when they had been carried to the sacred basilica, we had them placed, with exultation, upon the ceiling of the new structure, to the praise and glory of our Lord Jesus, Who protecting them from the hands of plunderers, had reserved them for Himself and the Holy Martyrs as He wished to do. Thus in this matter Divine generosity, which has chosen to limit and grant all things *according to weight and measure*, manifested itself as neither excessive nor defective; for not one more [timber] than was needed could be found.*

Medieval carpenters supported their buildings very cleverly; they strengthened them by underpinning, and, when altering the original plans, they also knew how to adapt the scaffolding most skilfully to the particular needs of the building. So when building the circular keep at Coucy with a diameter of 31.25 metres, they had the ingenious idea of building a spiral pathway with a very gentle slope around the wall. Little cartloads of materials could then be pulled up along this ramp.

Thirteenth-century miniatures show diminutive wheelbarrows of a simple

*English translation by Erwin Panofsky.

Two water mills: (*top*) stained glass from the Sainte Chapelle (thirteenth century, from Cluny Museum) and (*bottom*) manuscript of Herrade de Landsberg (twelfth century).

design which the carpenters made and which enabled one man to do the work of two labourers. This invention which was for a long time attributed to Pascal may well have been conceived by a humble carpenter during the 'cathedral crusade'.

As carpenters had to adapt themselves to new developments in vaulting, so the tilers had to adapt to the changing framework. The roofers and tilers, who worked in close collaboration with the carpenters, were men of considerable importance – it is recorded that one of them, Maître Pierre of Dijon, was lodged in Autun at the cathedral's expense. Roofing of large buildings was not habitual in classical times, but as the Middle Ages attained their fullest development in northern countries, adequate protection from rain and snow was imperative. Depending, therefore, on the region, churches were covered with tiles, lead or slate. Roman tiles were replaced by large flat tiles, and the lead roofing used in the early Middle Ages was made so that it was always possible to replace a damaged piece. At the end of the twelfth century, strong, solid slate was used in Western and Northern France. The ridges of the roofs, too, were beautifully decorated by the tilers. Paintings were applied to the metal by means of powerful fixatives, and the tilers took advantage of the fact that slate reflects light differently according to the way it is laid, to make two-tone mosaic patterns.

So as to protect the buildings from rain, the architects designed a network of guttering. They invented gargoyles to drain the water off away from the walls. For purposes of maintenance, passages were built at different levels and spiral staircases were improved. This also made it possible to move around the building in case of fire. Partly in order to lessen the risk of fire, architects took to building church vaults in stone, and to build these vaults they used methods which had been known in classical times, in Byzantium and the Orient, and produced barrel vaulting, groined vaulting and pendentives and squinches to support domes. They gradually improved their skills so that greater areas could be covered. They also thought of strengthening the groined vaulting by means of intersecting ribs which seem to have supported the weak spots along the joints and the highest points. We know now that intersecting rib vaulting, which the architects put to such good use, was a technological advance, but it did not have the prime importance which has so long been attributed to it. The experience of stonecutters, a better choice of materials and better mortar all contributed to the building of this type of vaulting which became common around the middle of the twelfth century.

The flying buttress was a revolutionary invention of the twelfth century which was used to support rib vaulting, thus making it possible to build taller and taller buildings. Flying buttresses were also used to prevent many old churches from falling down.

As the architects made ever larger windows so as to give more light, the glassmakers came to be among the most important cathedral builders. The

Top: There was no limit to the ambition and imagination of medieval engineers and technicians; yet of all their inventions the mechanical clock is perhaps the one which symbolizes their ultimate achievement. *Bottom:* The mechanical musical clock at Beauvais, perhaps the oldest in the world, was built between *1300* and *1321* by Canon Étienne Musique. Parts of the mechanism have been replaced throughout the centuries, and the clock case was built in the fifteenth century.

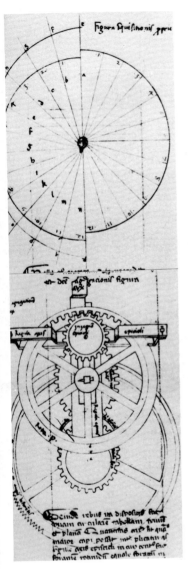

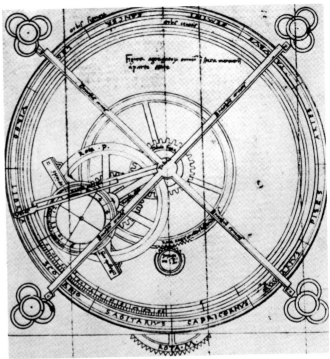

Between *1348* and *1360* in Padua, Giovanni di Dondi, doctor and astronomer, built an astronomical clock with seven dials. More than a century later, Leonardo da Vinci copied the dials of Venus and Mars when he was working in the library at Pavia where Dondi's clock was then kept.

Top left: (Dondi's drawing.) Diagram for an oval wheel.

Lower left: (Dondi's drawing.) Gearing with oval wheels and inward-facing teeth. Mechanism behind the Mercury dial.

Above right: (Dondi's drawing.) Mercury dial.

Opposite: Flying buttresses at Chartres Cathedral.

Flying buttresses at Mont Saint-Michel as seen by Viollet-le-Duc, *1835*.

making of stained glass is probably better understood than any other medieval technique, thanks to the monk Theophilus. He introduces himself as follows: 'I Theophilus, humble priest, servant of the servants of God, unworthy of the name and calling of "monk", hope that all those who wish to overcome the idleness of the spirit and the deviations of the heart by giving themselves up to useful manual work and to sweet meditation will be rewarded by a heavenly prize.'

Who would preface a technical treatise with such humility and faith these days? Theophilus continues:

When you have frequently re-read these things, when you have engraved them on your memory, and each time my book serves you well, in exchange for my advice I only ask that you offer a prayer to the Almighty that He take pity on my soul. He knows that I have not written down my precepts for love of worldly praise nor in hope of a reward here on earth, I have not withheld any valuable information through jealous spite, I have kept no secrets for myself alone, but I have wanted to supply the needs and help the progress of many men for the greater honour and glory of His name.

These moving extracts from the work of Theophilus help us to a better understanding of the spirit which moved the cathedral builders. A certain conception of progress, favourable social and economic conditions and a fruitful spirit of invention were all essential to the building of the cathedrals; equally, certain spiritual conditions were also needed before such miraculous churches as Notre-Dame de Paris and Notre-Dame de Chartres could be built. Because this is no place to deal with the subject, and because such a study would demand research outside the author's particular field, this must not be interpreted as a denial or an undervaluing of the part played by faith. The cathedrals bear witness not only to the ingenuity of science, but to an inspired wisdom, as the illustrations in this book go to prove.

The End of a World

The creative genius of the cathedral builders was dying away by the end of the thirteenth century; the people's enthusiasm for the 'cathedral crusade' had waned considerably. Builders were no longer motivated by the 'world-record' fever which had caused them with such passion to fling spires and naves higher and higher into the skies. Besides, the ultimate seemed to have been reached: the vault of Beauvais Cathedral, which was the highest in the world, fell down in 1284. Vivid colours gave way to subtler shades; stained glass began to be a thing of the past.

The faith which animated the 'cathedral crusade' was less ardent; the religious fervour which was so marvellous an inspiration to the Middle Ages in the ascendant, and which made them one of the greatest periods in the history of mankind, was to lose its intensity. Roger Bacon, who wrote an amazing treatise on educational reform which could have revivified medieval Christianity, was thrown into prison and died around 1292. Freedom of expression, which held a place of honour in universities, was stifled. Canon law clashed with Roman law, which was being revived, and nationalism put in an appearance. The Pope's authority and prestige declined. The great monastic orders founded no new abbeys and began to have difficulty in recruiting lay brothers.

The Bishop of Angers, Guillaume le Maire, has left an eloquent account of this religious crisis. This account is particularly significant because of the circumstances under which it was written. The Bishop had been asked by Pope Clement V to make a report on the religious situation in France for the Council of Vienna in 1311. He drew a dramatic picture:

In many parts of the kingdom of France an irreligious custom, or rather an abominable abuse, has been established. On Sundays and other important holy days dedicated to His Most Holy Majesty, when Christians should abstain from mercenary labour and attend divine service in church and hear from priests and others who are entitled to preach the word of God, of which they have such need – these days are chosen for fairs, trials and assizes. It even happens that the faithful, preferring the things of the flesh to those of the spirit, leave church services to meet in such places where they indulge in commerce or in legal matters. Consequently, on these holy days when God should be adored above all else, it is the Devil who is worshipped. The churches remain empty while law courts, taverns and workshops echo with quarrels, noise and blasphemy. Perjury and crimes of every kind are perpetrated. It follows from this that God's law, the articles of faith and all other things concerning the Christian religion and the salvation of the soul are completely overlooked by the faithful. God is blasphemed against. The Devil is revered, souls perish and the Catholic faith is wounded.

We might remember that this document was written by a man who distinguished himself by asking for the suppression of the Knights Templar. The decline of the holy army which St Bernard had praised was, in fact, a sign that the highest Christian possibilities had been exhausted. Although the condemnation of the Knights Templar was obtained by iniquitous means and for motives of self-interest, it resulted in part from a certain decline in the Order itself and was a glaring signal of the end of a world.

Religious and creative fervour died down, and at the same time the technological and economic boom came to a near-standstill. Most great medieval innovations date from before the end of the thirteenth century. For the next 150 years or so existing innovations were only improved upon, except in the military domain with the invention of the cannon in the fifteenth century. The magnificent prosperity of the thirteenth century was drawing to its close. Society began to set itself into a mould. The bourgeois produced by the first European industrial revolution, who because of their faith and civic sense had helped to finance hospitals and cathedrals, began to form dynasties and wanted to preserve the social *status quo*. They limited their gifts to the chapters. Communes ran into debt and, because of the royal centralization, lost some of their independence. The right to work and free enterprise, which had been responsible for the European economic boom, disappeared because of the trade corporations, which could be described as 'bosses exploiting a monopoly'. Sons succeeded their fathers and the best and cleverest no longer achieved positions of responsibility.

No more towns were founded. Land reclamation came to an end and the population was no longer growing. Inflation rapidly took a hold and nothing could stop it. During the Middle Ages there had always been devaluations, but it seems that the one which occurred under Philip the Fair at the beginning of the fourteenth century was felt particularly keenly. A charming song of 1313 reminds us of it:

Il se peut que le roy nous enchante;
Premier nous fit vingt de soixante,
Puis de vingt, quatre, et dix de trente.
. . . Or et argent tout est perdu,
Ne jamès n'en sera rendu.*

In 1337 the shattering collapse of the great Italian bank, Scali, announced the beginnings of the economic crisis which was to shake Europe.

The Hundred Years' War began in the same year and brought with it ruin and extreme poverty. Little by little most of the great French building sites were abandoned. Churches remained unfinished. War replaced faith, and when peace finally returned, more than a century later, only a handful of real builders were left in France. They managed to organize themselves into corporations, but these professional organizations remained isolated from one another. The German builders, on the other hand, who were not affected by the Hundred Years' War and the devastation it brought, and who continued to work on great cathedral sites, managed in relatively peaceful times to establish links between stonecutters' lodges in widely separated places.

In 1459 the master stonecutters met at Regensburg to standardize the statutes from the different lodges. So in the middle of the fifteenth century a vast organization of builders existed in Germany. It would appear that this organization reached its peak at around that time. Before the end of the fifteenth century the architect Roriczer had already broken with the association by publicly revealing a technique which the Regensburg gathering had wanted kept secret. In the sixteenth century the organization began to disintegrate. Until they finally disappeared in the seventeenth and eighteenth centuries, the German lodges were meeting-places for members of the trade.

In England and Scotland the lodges developed differently. Professional lodges evolved along the lines of speculative lodges. From the fifteenth century, but more so in the sixteenth and seventeenth centuries, English and Scottish masons allowed men who were not builders, but who were interested in the trade for various reasons, to attend their meetings and belong to their lodges. In this way 'operative masons' came to be distinguished from 'non-operative masons'. The first 'non-operative masons' who joined these professional lodges were, no doubt, clerks who had been put in charge of sites by the king, noblemen or the Church – for instance the clerk who drew up the Regius manuscript. Then sheriffs and mayors were allowed to join. Learned men with an interest in geometry were able to belong, so that they could study under the architects. Geometry was one of the seven liberal arts and therefore worthy of being learned and respected. Sometimes antiquarians joined these lodges,

*It seems the King enchants us: first he turns sixty into twenty, then twenty into four, and thirty into ten . . . gold and silver, all is lost – none of it will ever be returned.

wishing to study the architecture of the past, or in the hope of access to secrets of the past. The Regius and Cooke manuscripts, or variations on them which were read in the lodges, seemed to justify the interest of antiquarians in stone cutting and masonry, because these manuscripts described the cathedral builders as having their roots in earliest antiquity, and even claimed that they were descended from the builders of the temple of Solomon. D. Knoop and G.P. Jones have brilliantly analysed the sources of these legends. As often as not, they came straight from the Bible or from medieval writings.

Gradually more and more cultivated men or 'non-operative masons' and fewer and fewer workmen joined the lodges. It could be said that the history of English cathedral builders ended with the formation of the Grand Lodge in London in 1717. Then speculative freemasonry really began to flourish, and it has been rightly defined by D. Knoop and G. P. Jones as 'a particular system of ethics clouded by allegories and illustrated by symbols'.

The end of the French cathedral builders was less spectacular. During the sixteenth century they were to become building contractors to the Renaissance architects. At the end of the Hundred Years' War, the chapters, with admirable faith, attempted to inspire a new 'cathedral crusade', involving not only the handful of builders who had preserved the old traditions but indeed the whole population. And for about a hundred years, until the religious wars broke out, the canons determinedly tried, despite many material and spiritual difficulties, to finish the building of abandoned cathedrals. They were the worthy successors of the great canons of the twelfth and thirteenth centuries, but they did not seem to be aware that the world around them had changed radically; the builders were no longer those of the great age and the population lacked the faith which had inspired the men of an earlier era.

The initiative and invention which made the builders of the Middle Ages great no longer existed. The actions of the past were repeated mechanically, without faith or fervour. Builders could not move with their times and were stuck with old methods and the forms of bygone days; they were only capable of varying stone decorations on structure whose technique had been perfected two centuries earlier.

The builders organized themselves in guilds and were ceaselessly defending their rights and privileges, and thus managed to put a brake on the canons' enthusiasm. Some builders were so jealous of their prerogatives that they did not hesitate to go to the law to defend them. Some people spent more time in the law courts than on the building sites. And the best men did not necessarily become masters of the craft. The labourer could no longer cherish the hope of becoming a master, because inside the guilds sons succeeded their fathers, and nephews succeeded uncles. The chapters might well complain that these sons and nephews were gamblers, drunks or hooligans; they still had to resign themselves to employing them. In order to increase their powers, the guilds limited the number of masters, and the chapters were obliged to quarrel bitterly over the services of one architect.

The canons were disappointed in the builders, but even more so in the population's indifference to the house of God. The deep, uplifting faith of the twelfth and thirteenth centuries no longer inspired the soul nor inflamed the heart. Despite the foundation of new pious brotherhoods to raise funds, despite appeals from the Pope and indulgences granted to benefactors, despite the generosity of bishops and the subsidies of kings, the money collected was never enough for buildings to be completed. The people, without whom nothing on this scale can be accomplished, no longer replied to appeals for cathedrals. A contemporary report stated sadly and resignedly that the great undertakings of the past were no longer possible 'since charity has grown cold'.

Chronology

Bibliography

The memorandum of work carried out at the Augustinian convent (1299–1301) can be found in:
Fagniez, G., *Études sur l'industrie et la classe industrielle à Paris au XIIIe et au XIVe siècle*, Paris, 1877.

The account for the Saint-Lazare fabric at Autun for the year 1294–5 is in:
Quicherat, J., *Mélanges d'archéologie et d'histoire*, 2 vols., Paris, 1886.

The contract for the rebuilding of the church of the Cordeliers de Provins (1284) is in:
Mortet, V., *Un très ancien devis français*, Paris, 1897.

The accounts for Westminster Abbey are in:
Building Accounts of King Henry III, ed. H. M. Colvin, Oxford, Clarendon Press, 1971.

Many documents concerning the medieval French sites can be found in:
Mortet, V. and Deschamps, P., *Recueil des textes relatifs à l'histoire de l'architecture et à la condition des architectes en France au Moyen Age, XIe–XIIe siècle*, Paris, Picard, 1911. *XIIe–XIIIe siècle*, Paris, Picard, 1929.

On working conditions and building materials in England consult:
Salzman, L. F., *Building in England down to 1540*, Oxford, Clarendon Press, 1952.

The work which reawakened interest in medieval building sites is:
Knoop, D. and Jones, G. P., *The Medieval Mason*, Manchester U.P., 1967

Problems concerning building sites have subsequently been dealt with by:
Colombier, P. du, *Les chantiers des cathédrales*, Paris, Picard, 1973.
Gimpel, J., 'La liberté de travail et l'organisation des professions du bâtiment à l'époque des grandes constructions gothiques', *Revue d'histoire économique et sociale*, XXXIV, No. 3, 1956, pp. 303–14.
Aubert, M., 'La construction au Moyen Age', *Bulletin Monumental*, CXVIII, 1960, pp. 241–59; CXIX, 1961, pp. 7–42, 81–120, 181–209, 297–323; to be complemented by 'La construction au Moyen Age. Loges d'Allemagne, maçons et francs-maçons en Angleterre', ibid., CXVI, 1958, pp. 231–41.
The History of the King's Works, ed. H. M. Colvin, vol. 1, London, H.M.S.O., 1963.
Shelby, L. R., 'The Role of the Medieval Masons in Medieval English Buildings', *Speculum*, XXXIX, 1964, pp. 387–403.

Gonon, M., 'Comptes de construction en Forez au XIVe siècle', *La Construction au Moyen Age*, Paris, Les Belles Lettres, 1973, pp. 15–37.
David, M., 'La fabrique et les manoeuvres sur les chantiers des cathédrales de France jusqu'au XIVe siècle', *Études de droit, d'histoire du droit canonique dédiées à Gabriel Le Bras*, II, Paris, 1965.
Ravaux, J.-P., 'Les campagnes de construction de la cathédrale de Reims au XIIIe siècle', *Bulletin Monumental*, CXXXVII, 1979, pp. 8–59.

The masons', stonecutters', plasterers' and mortar makers' statute can be found in:
Lespinasse, R. de and Bonnardot, F., *Le livre des métiers d'Étienne Boileau*, Paris, 1879.

The register of the *taille* levied on Parisians in 1292:
Géraud, M., *Paris sous Philippe le Bel*, Paris, 1837.

On the working class in the Middle Ages:
Geremek, G., *Le salariat dans l'artisanat parisien aux XIIIe–XVe siècles*, Paris-La Haye, Mouton, 1968.
Martin Saint-Léon, E., *Histoire des corporations de métiers*, Paris, 1897; new edition, 1941.
Martin Saint-Léon, E., *Les Corporations en France avant 1789*, Paris, 1949.
Aclocque, G., *Les corporations, l'industrie et le commerce de Chartres*, Paris, 1917.

On the financing of the cathedrals:
Kraus, H., *Gold Was the Mortar: The Economics of Cathedral Building*, London, Routledge and Kegan Paul, 1979.
Biget, J. L., 'Recherche sur le financement des cathédrales du midi au XIIIe siècle', *La naissance et l'essor du gothique méridional au XIIIe siècle*, Cahiers de Fanjeaux, IX, Toulouse, Privat, 1974, pp. 124–64.
Vicaire, M. H., 'Le financement des jacobins de Toulouse: Conditions spirituelles et sociales des constructions (1229–1340)', ibid., pp. 209–53.
James, J., 'What Price the Cathedrals?', *Transactions of the Ancient Monuments Society*, XIX, 1972, pp. 47–65.

Suger's writings:
Abbot Suger on the Abbey Church of St. Denis and its Art Treasures, ed. and trans. E. Panofsky, Princeton, Princeton U.P., 1946.

Villard de Honnecourt's sketchbook:
Album de Villard de Honnecourt, manuscript published in facsimile, annotated by J. B. Lassus, Paris, 1858; new edition, Paris, Laget, 1968.
Villard de Honnecourt – Kritische Gesamtausgabe des Bauhüttenbuches, R. Hahnloser, Vienna, 1935.

The Sketchbook of Villard de Honnecourt, ed. Th. Bowie, Bloomington, Indiana U.P., 1959.

On architects' techniques:

Architector: *The Lodge Books and Sketchbooks of Medieval Architects*, ed. F. Bucher, New York, Abaris, 1979.

Viollet-le-Duc, E., *Dictionnaire raisonné de l'architecture française du XIe au XVIe siècle*, Paris 1858–68, new ed., 10 vols., Paris, Sancey, 1979. (The following chapters are particularly useful: armature – chainage – charpente – construction – échafaud – engin – escalier – étai – galerie – voûte.)

Gimpel, J., 'Sciences et techniques des maitres-maçons du XIIIe siècle', *Techniques et civilisations*, II, 5–6 (1953), pp. 147–51.

Fitchen, J., *The Construction of Gothic Cathedrals: A Study of Medieval Vault Erection*, Oxford, Clarendon Press, 1961.

Kimpel, D., 'Le développement de la taille en série dans l'architecture médiévale et son rôle dans l'histoire économique', *Bulletin Monumental*, CXXXV (1977), pp. 195–222.

On the origins of freemasonry:

Knoop, D. and Jones, G. P., *The Genesis of Freemasonry*, Manchester, Manchester U.P., 1949.

Knoop, D., Jones, G. P. and Hamer, D., *The Two Earliest Masonic MSS*, Manchester, Manchester U.P., 1938.

On the history of technology and medieval science:

Gille, B., 'Le moulin à eau, une révolution technique médiévale', *Techniques et Civilisations*, III, Paris, 1954.

'Le Moyen Age', *Histoire des Techniques*, ed. B. Gille, Encyclopédie de La Pléiade, Paris, Gallimard, 1978, pp. 508–79.

Gimpel, J., *La révolution industrielle du Moyen Age*, coll. Points Histoire, Paris, Éd. du Seuil, 1975.

White, L., Jr., *Technologie médiévale et transformations sociales*, Paris-La Haye, Mouton, 1969.

White, L., Jr., *Medieval Religion and Technology: Collected Essays*, California, U.C.L.A., 1979.

Crombie, A. C., *Histoire des sciences de saint Augustin à Galilée, 400–1650*, vol. 1, Paris, PUF, 1957.

Beaujouan, G., 'La science dans l'occident médiéval chrétien', *Histoire générale des sciences*, I, Paris, PUF, 1957.

Beaujouan, G., 'Calcul d'expert, en 1391, sur le chantier du dôme de Milan', *Le Moyen Age*, LXIX (1963), pp. 555–63.

Particularly recommended on life in the Middle Ages:

Pernoud, R., *Pour en finir avec le Moyen Age*, coll. Points Histoire, Paris, Éd. du Seuil, 1979.

Pernoud, R., *Histoire de la bourgeoisie en France*, coll. Points Histoire, Paris, Éd. du Seuil, 1980, 2 vols.

Pirenne, H., *Histoire économique et sociale du Moyen Age*, Paris, PUF, 1969.

Petit-Dutaillis, Ch., *Les communes françaises*, Paris, 1947.

Mollat, M., *Genèse médiévale de la France moderne, XIVe–XVe siècle*, Paris, Arthaud, 1974.

Delort, R., *Le Moyen Age; histoire illustrée de la vie quotidienne*, Lausanne, Edita, 1972.

Duby, G. and Walton, A., edd., *Histoire de la France rurale*, I–II, Paris, Éd. du Seuil, 1975.

Branner, R., 'Three Problems from the Villard de Honnecourt Manuscript', *Art Bulletin*, XXXIX (1957), pp. 61–7.

Branner, R., 'Villard de Honnecourt, Archimedes and Chartres', *Journal of the Society of Architectural Historians*, XIX (1960), pp. 91–6.

Barnes, C. F., Jr., *The Drawings of Villard de Honnecourt: A Critical Bibliography of Sources and Studies, 1661–1981*, Boston, Hall, 1981.

Shelby, L. R., 'Medieval Masons' Templates', *Journal of the Society of Architectural Historians*, XXX (1971), pp. 140–54.

Shelby, L. R., *Gothic Design Technics: The Fifteenth-Century Design Booklets of Mathias Roriczer and Hans Schmuttermayer*, Carbondale, Illinois U.P., 1977.

Harvey, J., 'The Tracing Floor in York Minster', *40th Annual Report of the Friends of York Minster*, 1968.

Bucher, F., 'Design in Gothic Architecture: A Preliminary Assessment', *Journal of the Society of Architectural Historians*, XXXVII (1968), pp. 49–71.

Fergusson, P. J., 'Notes on Two Cistercian Engraved Designs', *Speculum*, LIV (1979).

Sené, A., 'Un instrument de précision au service des artisans du Moyen Age: l'équerre', *Cahiers de civilisation médiévale*, XIIIe année, 1970, pp. 349–58.

Consult on English and French architects:

Lance, A., *Dictionnaire des architectes français*, Paris, 1872.

Lefèvre-Pontalis, E., 'Répertoire des architectes, maçons sculpteurs, charpentiers et ouvriers français au XIe et au XIIe siècle', *Bulletin Monumental*, LXXV (1911), pp. 423–68.

Harvey, J., *English Medieval Architects: A Biographical Dictionary down to 1550, including Master Masons, Carpenters, Carvers, Building Contractors and Others Responsible for Design*, London, Batsford 1954.

Harvey, J., *Henri Yevele, c. 1320–1400: The Life of an English Architect*, London, Batsford, 1944.

Study of models in polarized light:

Mark, R. and Prentke, R. A., 'Model analysis of Gothic Structure', *Journal of the Society of Architectural Historians*, XXVII (1968), pp. 44–8.

Mark, R. and Jonash, R. S., 'Wind Loading on Gothic Structure', *Journal of the Society of Architectural Historians*, XXIX (1970), pp. 222–30.

On proportions and medieval aesthetics:

Ackerman, J. S., 'Ars Sine Scientia Nihil Est: Gothic Theory of Architecture at the Cathedral of Milan', *Art Bulletin*, XXXI (1949), pp. 24–111.

Schapiro, M., 'On the Aesthetic Attitude in Romanesque Art', *Art and Thought in Honour of Dr. A. K. Coomaraswamy*, London, 1947, pp. 130–50.

Frankl, P., *The Gothic Literary Sources and Interpretations through Eight Centuries*, Princeton, Princeton U.P., 1960.

De Bruyne, E., *Études d'esthétique médiévale*, 3 vols., Bruges, Detemple, 1946.

Index

statutes, guilds, 60, 77, 79, 102; Boileau's
compilation, 60, 61–2, 65, 67, 79,
108–9; legends of, 2; privileges, 152–3;
Roriczer, 101, 151; *and see* secrecy in
guilds
stonecutters, stoneworkers, *see* lodges; marks;
masons
Strasbourg Cathedral (Bas-Rhin), 27, 77;
elevations, 117, *118, 119*; rose window,
112, 113; spire, 2
Suger (Abbot of St-Denis and author,
1081–1151): and St-Denis, 9–18, 27,
139–40, *10, 12, 13, 19*
Sunday labour, 149

taxes, *taille, 32, 54, 62–5, 120
technological advances, 133–47, 150,
152
theologians, and sculptors, 85, 86
Theophilus (12th c. monk), 147
tidemills, 134
tilers, 142
timber, *92, 96, 139–40, 99, 138*
tools, 136–7, *40, 44, 64, 73, 136*
Tours Cathedral (Indre-et-Loire): interior
whitewashed, 23; relics, 56
town halls, churches used as, 41
town planning (11th–13th c.), *29, 30, 42–3,*
121, 150
towns, models of, *93*
tracing houses, 115
transport of materials, 30, 82, 87; Autun,
55, 59, 69; Hérault, 121; Paris, 59
treadwheel, *96, 97, 135*
Trent, Council of (South Tyrol, 1545–63),
49

United States compared with medieval
Europe, 30, 32, 59, 62
Uppsala Cathedral (Sweden), 78

Vale Royal (Cheshire, 13th c. Cistercian
abbey), 41, 69, 77
Vézelay Abbey: sculpture, 82, 86
Villard de Honnecourt (13th c. French
architect and craftsman), 123, 124;
comparison with Giotto, *106, 107;*

Villard de Honnecourt *(cont'd)*
comparison with 20th c. US architects,
62; sketchbook, 89–102, 117, 123, 139,
88, 90, 93, 95, 96, 99, 102, 106
Viollet-le-Duc, Eugène-Emanuel (French
architect and author, 1814–79), *viii,* 2,
146
Virgin Mary, *see* Marian cult; Notre-Dame
Vitruvius, Marcus (1st c. BC Roman
architect, author of *De Architectura*),
106–7
voluntary work, 2, 60, 131

Wachsmann, Konrad (20th c. US architect),
62
wages, 41–2, 54–6, 59–60, 62, 66–70, 92,
120
Walters, Frederick (20th c. English
architect), 131
watch, exemptions from the, 62
water mills, waterwheels, *see* hydraulic
power
Westminster Abbey (London), 137; accounts
and statistics, 56, 67, 68, 120; sculpture,
110
wheelbarrow invented, 140, 142
whitewashing in churches, 18, 23
William of Sens (12th c. architect and
craftsman), 123–4, 126
winches, *96, 97,* 124
Winchester Cathedral (Hampshire): bishop
and chapter, 49; relics, 57
windmills, 134
windows, larger, 142
women workers, 64
wood-cutting under water, *96, 99*
wooden buildings, 7–8
"world record" fever (13th c. and 20th c.),
32, 36, 149, *34, 35*
Wright, Frank Lloyd (US architect,
1869–1959), 62

Yale University: excavations at St-Denis,
107–8
York Minster: chapter statutes (1352), 77,
79; 14th c. tracing house, 115;
rebuilding in 1970s, *48, 58*

Illustration Sources

Archives photographiques, 146
Archives Seuil, 16, 39b, 44a, 71a, 90, 103, 130, 143b, 144
Bibliothèque Nationale, 40b, 44b, 50, 51, 53, 57, 88, 93, 95, 96, 99, 102, 106, 141b, 148
Jacques Boulas, 66
Boudot-Lamotte, 122
British Library, 83b, 85
Claude Caroly, 26
Centre de recherche sur les monuments historiques, 113
Compagnons du Devoir, 138a, 138b, 139
Dean and Chapter of Westminster, 110a, 110b
Dijon Library, 97
Éditions Picard, 82, 116a, 116b, 116c
Fotogram/Favreau, 63
Fotogram/Stanimirovitch, 80
Fotogram/Unwin, viii
Garanger, 29, 37b, 71b, 74, 81, 145
Giraudon, frontispiece, 40a, 43
Hidalgo, 35
Houvet, 47
Michel Langrognet, 76
J.-R. Masson, 6, 10, 15, 19, 20, 21, 22, 61, 127
Musée de l'Oeuvre, Strasbourg, 91, 125a, 135
Musée de l'Outil, Troyes (photos: Chevalier), 64, 73, 136
National Library, Vienna, 91, 125a, 135
Patrimoine National (Real Casa, Madrid), 83a, 125b
Réunion des Musées Nationaux, 12, 13, 141a
Roubier, 33, 112
Émile Rousset, 34, 36, 73a, 143a
John Rylands Library, 39a
Scala, 107
Shepherd Building Group Ltd, 48, 58
Stadtarchiv, Cologne, 105
Top/Mennesson, 31
Top/Reichel, 70
Jean Vigne, 132
Roger Viollet, 87
Yan, 46, 78

growth of Marian cult
age of great theologans: Aquinas, Abelard, St. Francis
growth of monastic order; Benedictine, Cluny
growth of cities, commerce, wealth
birth of bourgois & civil liberties
   economic develop. thru free enterprise; bankers + industrialist
develop. of free towns - local patriotism
prosperity - guilt - charity
replace Crusades as expiation for sins
some clerics ~~shr~~ shocked at ostentation
all classes gathered together & had had the same education
   + so same symbols understanding - unity
Chapter with dean over canons (priests) powerful +
   challenged bishops sometimes - allowed to live
   independently, oversaw building, separate incomes
      raised money
         traveling relics prayer for dead
         indulgences
         bishops
         tax selves   -
100 yrs. war